Bon Appétit

French–English Menu Dictionary

JUDITH A. WHITE

ROBERT HALE · LONDON

© *Judith A. White 1998*
First published in Great Britain 1998

ISBN 0 7090 6285 0

Robert Hale Limited
Clerkenwell House
Clerkenwell Green
London EC1R 0HT

2 4 6 8 10 9 7 5 3 2 1

Typeset in North Wales by
Derek Doyle & Associates, Mold, Flintshire
Printed in Great Britain by
St Edmundsbury Press Limited, Bury St Edmunds
and bound by
WBC Book Manufacturers Limited, Bridgend

Contents

Introduction

My admiration for the way in which the French enjoy their food has no bounds. Meal times are occasions – the French rarely indulge in hurried snacks, squashy sandwiches or damp food from lunch-boxes. The 'school-dinners' atmosphere of staff canteens or high street 'caffs' is hardly known in France – thank goodness. French cuisine is one of the reasons I enjoy visiting France so much – every meal, however humble, is prepared with care; attention is paid to every tiny detail.

Nothing frustrates me more than to try to choose a meal from a menu which I do not understand. I am always sure that I am missing some superb gastronomic experience – this often results in my ordering something by name alone and, occasionally, I find it is one of the few foods I do not wish to eat. My knowledge of French is reasonable but I decided that, to eat really well, I needed to know more than simple, basic French. So often dictionaries have failed me – understandably they cannot include every word in the language and must concentrate on those needed most often.

With so many different dishes, garnishes and ways of cooking the only solution was to write my own dictionary. I hope that this little book will be as useful to anyone referring to it as it has already been to me. With it to hand, I hope you will have the courage to try new dishes, having a basic idea of what they are before you order, safe in the knowledge that you can avoid anything you may find distasteful or to which you are allergic.

All items mentioned in the dictionary are eaten in some part of France although we in Britain would not always consider them edible. I have only given the gastronomic meanings of words, even where there may be several other meanings. My dictionary is not a grammar so I have omitted definite articles.

Throughout the areas in which French cooking is used, there

are so many different cooking methods, garnishes, available ingredients, etc., that it would be impossible to include them all. I hope that I have listed all the main words you will come across – some of them may not be French but are used frequently in French menus. If there are any glaring omissions or errors, I am sure someone will tell me!

This is not a recipe book. For compound dishes the main ingredients have been listed but their quantities may vary from region to region and kitchen to kitchen. Traditional ingredients have been given where possible but I cannot be responsible for the vagaries of chefs who may wish to take the classic names and put them to their own dishes with quite different ingredients. The meanings of some words or phrases may also vary from area to area, for instance *coque* means cockle in the North of France but *coque du Lot* means a special Easter cake in the Lot area.

Wine names and types have not been included as they are so extensive as to need a book of their own. However, I have included a list of basic drinks and also some where they are commonly used in recipes.

In some parts of the English text, I have used French words in preference to English. This is solely to avoid confusion – for instance the English word 'pastry' can mean the dough used to make tarts, pies, etc., or a little cake made from that dough. In this case, to avoid ambiguity, I have used the French 'patisserie' when I mean a small cake or pastry.

I hope you enjoy my dictionary – do let me know if you think there are any ways in which it could be improved.

Judith A. White
Ely, Cambridgeshire, England

How to Use the Dictionary

Basically, the Gastronomic Dictionary should be used as you would use any dictionary but there are a few points to be noted:

1) Compound phrases are written with a comma following the indexed word if the indexed word is not the first word of the phrase:
   e.g. *Florence, consommé* would appear on menus as *Consommé Florence* whereas *pommes purée* will appear as such on menus.
2) St., Saint and Sainte are all included in alphabetical order under 'Saint'.
3) Where the same word or phrase has more than one meaning, these are separated by a semi-colon,
   e.g. *chevrette* = a cheese from the Savoy area; a roebuck; a shrimp.
4) For most entries, it is necessary to look up both the adjective and the noun if neither is known,
   e.g. *oeufs durs*: *oeufs* = eggs, *durs* = hard-boiled.

However, some foods are given with adjectives where these are very common and you could also find *oeufs durs* under *oeufs* following *oeufs brouillés*.

I have used this system for some soups, sauces, vegetables and a few other categories. I hope this will be found helpful and time-saving.

Eating Out in France

French eating habits vary considerably from those of the British. Full meals are served at set times – usually 12–2 for lunch and 7–10 for dinner. Some smaller hotels and restaurants will tell you that dinner is served at 7.30 – if you arrive at 7.40 you could find all the tables full!

Between these set meal times you will be able to eat simple meals at brasseries or snacks at some cafés – a *croque-monsieur* (a toasted cheese and ham sandwich), an omelette, a plate of cold sausage or a substantial sandwich.

Never be put off by the apparent unprepossessing external appearance of a restaurant. Look inside and you are sure to see clean, beautifully-laid tables with shining cutlery and glasses and dishes of crisp, sliced French bread. The sight alone is enough to give you an appetite!

When eating in a restaurant, you will be offered either *La carte* (an à la carte menu) or *le menu* which is a choice of two or three or more set menus. Both *la carte* and *le menu* will always be displayed outside the restaurant so you know before you go in if that restaurant will suit you.

Le menu is invariably the best value. Even the simplest will consist of three courses, each with two or three choices. *Menus touristiques* are to be avoided if possible as they are usually constructed with the restaurateur's view of what he considers the tourist will want to eat. I have found that his views rarely correspond with mine on this point! *Menus gastronomiques* are usually also excellent value, offering the best of the local ingredients and regional dishes at realistic prices.

In some restaurants, you may find a *menu rapide* or *formule rapide* – this is, as its name suggests, a quick, basic meal. It is generally aimed at office workers with only a scant hour for lunch and usually consists of two courses, speedily served – excellent for a mid-day stop if you are expecting a real feast in the evening or if you are facing a full afternoon's driving to your next stopping-place!

However, between these two are many excellent value menus with almost as wide a choice as an à la carte menu would offer. The majority of restaurants will have three or four, sometimes more, fixed price menus which could range from a very inexpensive two course meal (say 40F or 50F) to a five or six course meal with a selection of very special dishes at perhaps 200F or more. Each diner chooses the menu he prefers and, before ordering, tells the waiter which price menu he has selected. Several people eating together can, if they wish, all choose from different menus. The waiters are used to this and will sort it out most efficiently.

The price of the *menu fixe* is for one choice from each course shown and there is no reduction should you wish to omit a course. Menus usually consist of an hors d'oeuvre course, a fish course, a meat course and a dessert or cheese course. In France, the cheese is usually served before the dessert, not after as in Britain, and you will probably be offered an amazing array of local and national cheeses of all sorts. Do not be afraid to ask what each is – the waiter will know and will take pride in pointing out which are the local cheeses. You will be expected to make a choice of two or three and may even be invited to help yourself rather than be served by the waiter.

Coffee is always charged as an extra but the menu price sometimes includes a glass of house wine (*'boisson compris'*) and more often than not will include a 15 per cent service charge, (*'service compris'*). If this is not so (*'service non compris'*), it is customary to leave a tip of 15–20 per cent.

The house wines are nearly always good value, as the French customers will frequently drink these and they would not tolerate a wine which was not of reasonable quality for the price. House wines are served either by the glass, by the quarter, half or full carafe. However, do not feel obliged to drink if you do not wish to do so. A carafe of fresh water or a bottle of spa water will always be willingly provided if it is requested.

Finally, two warnings.

First, remember that Sunday lunchtimes are the French family

meal times and a great many restaurants will be fully booked –
therefore, find somewhere to eat as early as possible!

Secondly, never be in a hurry over a meal in a restaurant. Even
a straightforward three-course meal will usually take an hour or
more – the French expect you to sit over the meal, discussing its
merits at length and putting the world to rights between courses.
The 'rush in, eat, rush out and get on with the day' syndrome is
unknown in France – and long may it be so!

Summary of the Regional Culinary Differences

Alsace

There is a strong German influence in the food of Alsace with the emphasis on hearty stews, charcuterie of all sorts, and solid desserts and pastries. Pork, in all its forms, is the favoured meat, and vegetables are an important part of every meal.

Specialities to look for:
Schifela (shoulder of pork with pickled turnips); beckenoffe (a stew with lamb, pork, beef, onions and potatoes cooked in a local wine); Strasbourg black puddings; choucroute (pickled cabbage cooked with ham, pork and Strasbourg sausages); matelote (an eel stew, sometimes with other fish); bilberry tart; Kugelhopf (brioche with almonds and raisins)

Cheeses Carré de l'Est (soft, mild, square); Munster (stronger-flavoured, disc-shaped)
Wines   Riesling; Muscat; Tokay d'Alsace; Gewurtztraminer

Brittany

Renowned for its fish and shellfish. The cream and butter produced here are superb, as are the salt-meadow sheep. The duckling from Nantes and the wide variety of game are famous.

Specialities to look for:
Agneau de pré-salé (sheep from the salt marshes of Brittany); cotriade (fish soup with potatoes, onions and garlic); charcuterie; bardatte (cabbage stuffed with hare); galette (biscuit, cake or

pancake – may be sweet or savoury); crêpes (may be sweet or savoury); blé noir (buckwheat); palourdes farcies (stuffed clams); far breton (batter with raisins); gâteau breton (flavoured with rum)

Cheeses	Campénéac (strong, uncooked); Port Salut (semi-hard, mild); St Paulin
Wines	Muscadet

Burgundy

The cuisine of Burgundy is the best in France – at the same time robust but delicate. Burgundy is known for Charolais, the famous white cattle, the poultry of Bresse, its abundant fish and, of course, Dijon mustard. Meat stews and braised meats are complemented with rich wines or cream sauces. Both fish and meat dishes are often garnished with mushrooms and many types of onions. Poultry is raised and respected throughout Burgundy – coq au vin originated here.

Specialities to look for:
Boeuf bourguignon; garbure (a thick soup with pork, sausages, cabbage and beans); pochouse (fish stew with garlic); daube aux poireaux; escargots à la crème; quenelles de brochet (pike); nonettes de Dijon; flamusse bressane

Cheeses	Langres (strong, cone-shaped); époisses (soft, mild, flat); Montrachet (soft, creamy, cylindrical goat cheese); Rouy (strong square)
Wines	Gevrey-Chambertin; Volnay; Pommard; Santenay; Passetoutgrains; Bourgogne Aligoté
	Try kir – cassis de Dijon with sharp white Bourgogne Aligoté

Champagne–Ardennes

The cuisine of this area is excellent if somewhat limited. Charcuterie is superb, as is the locally raised lamb and poultry. Freshwater fish, such as carp, pike, salmon and trout are succulent and plentiful, and game also abounds.

Specialities to look for:
Boudin de lapin (steamed rabbit pudding); flamiche aux Maroilles (cheese tart); waterzoi (thick soup of fish or chicken); andouillettes (chitterling sausages); sanguette (black pudding); langues fourrées (pressed tongues)

Cheeses	Chaumont (strong, soft, cone-shaped); Brie; Coulommiers (soft, creamy); Maroilles (soft, salty); Chaource (creamy, mild, cylinder-shaped)
Wines	Champagne; Crémant de Cramant; Bouzy; Bisseuil; Vin Gris; Rosé des Riceys

Dordogne

An area rich in fresh fruit and vegetables. Poultry of all kinds are reared here and pâté de fois gras, Confit de canard and cou d'oie (stuffed goose neck) are world famous. But the main pride of the area is the truffle. All dishes called 'à la périgourdine' include a garnish of truffles and/or pâté de fois gras.

Specialities to look for:
Confit de canard; pâté de fois gras; chou farci; truffles and cèpes; cou d'oie; friands de Bergerac (small potato cakes); mique (stew or soup with dumplings); tourin bordelais or ouillat (onion soup); merveilles (sugar-coated fritters)

Cheeses	Bleu d'Auvergne (strong, blue); cantal (semi-hard, nutty flavour); fourme d'Ambert (cylinder-shaped, blue); roquefort; cabécou de Rocamadour (tiny, nutty, made from goats' milk)
Wines	Bergerac; Pécharmant; Gaillac mousseux; Côtes de Duras

Flanders, The North

The cuisine of Flanders is similar to that of Picardy. The food is robust, filling, yet varied. Stews and casseroles of all sorts are the staple foods, as are waffles, pancakes and batter dishes. Be sure to try 'cheval' – the strong-flavoured horse meat!

Specialities to look for:
Andouilles/ettes; tripe; pâtés; all fish, both from sea and river –
especially herring, eels, oysters; hochepot du nord; sanguette;
soupe courquignoise (with fish, moules, leeks and cheese);
croquelots de Dunkirk (herrings smoked with hazel leaves);
carbonnade flamande; waterzoi; croquelins du Roubaix; red plum
tart; waffles with cherries

Cheeses Maroilles (soft, salty); Gris de Lille (strong, salty);
Boulette de Cambrai (herb-flavoured, ball-shaped)
Wines Beer and gin-based drinks are favoured in this region.

Languedoc–Roussillon

The cuisine of this area can be robust but many delicate dishes
have originated here. Fine game and poultry are raised and menus
always offer a varied selection of saltwater and freshwater fish.
Tomatoes, peppers, courgettes and aubergines feature promi-
nently, together with herbs and garlic.

Specialities to look for:
Pâté de fois gras with truffles; Cargolade (snails stewed in wine);
boles de picoulat (beef and pork balls with tomatoes and garlic); aigo
bouido (garlic soup); boutifare (bacon and herb pudding); brandade
of cod; fricandeau de thon à la catalane (tuna with olives and/or
anchovies); touron (pastry with almonds, other nuts and fruit)

Cheeses Les orrys (strong, disc-shaped); pélardon (goats'-milk
cheese, soft texture, nutty flavour); Montségur (bland,
disc-shaped)
Wines Château de Levrette; Clos Val-Marie Romanée; Cruzy;
Minervois; Corbières Supérieur; Picpoul; Grenache du
Château de Serame

Loire

The Loire Valley is abundant with fish – salmon, trout, chad, eels
and pike among others. Pork is the favoured meat (les rilleaux

d'Anjou are well-known), poultry, venison and baby goat are delicious. Game is plentiful, dishes using rabbit and hare are most inventive and use large quantities of fresh herbs. All vegetables prosper in the rich soil, as do fruits. Pears, apples and prunes are freely used.

Specialities to look for:
Beuchelle à la Tourangelle (kidneys, sweetbreads, morels, truffles and cream); bardette (stuffed cabbage); biquet en pot (goat casserole); alose à l'oseille (shad with a sorrel sauce); bourdaines (jam-filled baked apples); gâteau Pithiviers (almond paste pie); Amandin aux Belles Angevines (pears with almond meringue).

Cheeses	Olivet bleu (small, fruity blue cheese); Frinault (small, soft); St Paulin (firm, mild, yellow in colour); crottin de Chavignol (goats'-milk cheese); selles-sur-Cher (white, mild goats'-milk cheese with blue skin); Crémets (fresh cream cheese eaten with sugar and cream).
Wines	Touraine; Vouvray; Bonnezeaux (all sweet); Sancerre; Quincy; Côteaux de l'Aubance; Gamay de Touraine; rosé de Bué

Lorraine

The cuisine of Lorraine is similar to that of Alsace but the influence is Polish rather than German. The dishes are very substantial and filling.

Specialities to look for:
Beckenoffe (a lamb and pork casserole); potée (a robust soup); potage Lorrain (soup with potatoes, leeks, bacon and onions); Quiche Lorraine (made with eggs, cream and lean bacon); tourte à la Lorraine (with pork and veal); potted meats; black puddings; Mirabelle plum tart; Nancy cake; bergamot pastries

Cheeses	Gérardmer (made from scalded curds); Fromgey (soft, spreading cheese)
Wines	Château-Salins; Vir; pineau de Bar; Vaucouleurs; Sarrebourg; Essey-la-Côte; Bruley

Normandy

An area of high gastronomic repute. Excellent butter and cream are produced here and are used liberally. Cattle and sheep, especially salt-meadow sheep, provide high quality meat. Charcuterie, fish, and shellfish are plentiful. Fruit production is important and apples appear in many menus. Apples are used to make cidre bouché (sparkling cider) and Calvados, a distilled apple brandy.

Specialities to look for:
Tripes à la mode de Caen; ficelle Normande (pancake stuffed with ham, mushrooms and cheese); barbue au cidre (brill cooked in cider); trou Normand (a between-course sorbet with calvados); Seine (shad stuffed and baked); cassolette de Saint-Jacques à la normande (scallops cooked with cream and calvados); canard au sang à la rouennaise (duck cooked with its giblets, cream and calvados); bourdelots (baked apples in pastry)

Cheeses Livarot (semi-hard, strong); Pont l'Eveque (rectangular, strong, soft); carré de Bray (small, square, mild); Camembert

Wines There are no vineyards in this region, and wine is not much drunk here – Cidre bouché (sparkling cider) and Calvados are preferred. Bénédictine is distilled at Fécamp.

Provence

A region of garlic, herbs, tomatoes, peppers, aubergines and courgettes. Ratatouille, aïoli, pistou and pissaladière appear in some form on most menus. Production of high quality meat is not attempted in this arid climate; beef must be cooked long and slowly – 'à la daube'; fish stews (bourride, bouillabaisse) are popular, as are mussels, salt cod and mullet.

Specialities to look for:
Aigo-sacu (fish soup with garlic); red mullet with fennel; sartada-gagnano (macédoine of little fish, pressed and fried); esquinado de Toulon (crabs and mussels); gayettes (sausages of pig's liver); soufassum (stuffed cabbage with mutton); bugnes d'Arles

Cheeses   Brousse du Rove (mild ewe's-milk cheese); picodon de Valréas (soft, nutty, goats'-milk cheese); Mont-Ventoux (strong, soft)

Wines   Château Simone; Bellet; Château Vignelaure; Tavel rosé; Châteauneuf-du-Pape; Roquevaire; Condrieu; Gigondas; Rasteau; Crozes-Hermitage; Côtes du Rhône

Abatis or abattis	giblets
abats	offal
Abbayé d'Entrammes	a soft cream cheese
abdelavis	Jerusalem melon (very sweet melon originating in Jerusalem)
ablette	bleak, a freshwater fish
abricot	apricot
abricoté	candied apricot; apricot flavoured
abricots Bourdaloue	with semolina and kirsch; with almonds and macaroons
abricots Colbert	apricots poached in vanilla syrup
absinthe	pastis: aniseed-flavoured aperitif
acajou, noix d'	cashew nut
acanthe	acanthus (usually eaten as a salad)
acarne	sea bream
acavé	variety of snail
accolade, en	served 'back to back' on the same dish
accuniatu	Corsican stew with lamb or goats' meat
aceline	perch-like fish
acerbe	tart, sour
acétoselle	wood sorrel
achards	vegetable pickles
âche	wild celery
achigan	(black) bass
acide	tart, sour
actinie	sea anemone
admirable jaune	orange-tinted variety of peach
aettekees	a Belgian cheese
africaine, à l'	with black potato balls (made from

	potatoes with blue-black flesh) and courgettes
africaine, sauce	brown sauce with onions, tomatoes and peppers
agneau	lamb
agneau de lait	milk-fed lamb, yeanling
agneau pré-salé	lamb raised on salt marshes
agnelet	baby lamb
Agnès Sorel	salpicon of tongue, rice and mushrooms
agoursi	ridge cucumber
agrumes	citrus fruits
Aïda, salade	with chicory, tomatoes, artichoke hearts, pimiento and hard-boiled eggs
aiglefin	haddock
aiglon	poached apricots, peaches and nectarines
aigo à la ménagère	soup with onions, leeks, saffron and orange peel
aigo bouido or boulido	soup with poached eggs and garlic
aigo-saou	a fish soup from Provence
aigre de cèdre	citrus fruit drink
aigre-doux	sweet-and-sour
aigrefin	haddock
aïgroissade	chick peas with aïoli, beans and potatoes
aiguillat	dog-fish
aiguillette	very thin slice of meat, usually breast
aiguillette de boeuf	thin slice of topside
ail	garlic
ail, chapon à l'	uncooked garlic bread eaten with salad
aile	wing
aileron	wing-tip
aillade	garlic sauce
aillade, pain à l'	slice of toasted garlic bread
aillé	garlic-flavoured
ailloli or aïoli	mayonnaise with pounded garlic
airelle	cranberry; whortleberry; huckleberry
airelle coussinette	cranberry
airelle myrtille	bilberry

albacore	type of tunny fish
albarelle	variety of edible fungus
alberge	clingstone peach or apricot
Albert, sauce	made with horseradish and mustard and cream
albigeoise	with croquette potatoes and stuffed tomatoes
albigeoise, pot au feu	stew with stuffed goose-neck
albigeoise, soupe	with beef, pork, sausage and goose
alboni, sauce	made with game stock and juniper berries
albran	halbran, wild duck
albuféra	with truffles and forcemeat balls
alcazar	almond flavoured meringue tart
alcool	alcohol
alcool blanc	fruit brandy
alénois	garden cress
algérienne	with tomatoes and croquette potatoes or rice
algue	seaweed
Ali Baba, salade	with sweet potatoes, hard-boiled eggs, shrimps, courgettes and tomatoes
alicot or alicuit	stew of giblets from Languedoc
aligot	potato and cheese purée
alise	sorb-apple
allemande	with noodles and/or mashed potatoes
allemande, salade	with boiled potatoes, apples, beetroot, onions, salt herrings and gherkins
allemande, sauce	classic white sauce made from eggs and cream
allumettes	matchstick-shaped; pastry straws
allumettes, pommes	matchstick-shaped fried potatoes
alma	(of fruits) poached in port
almina	tangerines with bavarois
aloès	aloes
alose	shad
alouette	lark
alouette de mer	sea-lark, summer snipe, type of plover
alouettes sans tête	stuffed escalopes, usually of veal
aloumère	a type of mushroom

aloyau	the entire sirloin
alphée	a crayfish-like crustacean
alsacienne	with foie gras; with sauerkraut and frankfurters; with artichoke hearts, mushroom purée and horseradish
alsacienne, salade	with apples, potatoes, onions, truffles, walnuts
amandes	almonds
amandes amères	bitter almonds
amandes béraudes	broad, fleshy almonds
amandes brutes	shelled, unblanched almonds
amandes salées	salted almonds
amandes Tournefort	small, strongly-flavoured almonds
amandine	almond-flavoured
ambassadrice	with mushrooms and chickens' livers
Ambert, fourme d'	a fruity flavoured blue cheese from Auvergne
ambrette	ambergris-flavoured pear
améléon	type of cider from Normandy
amer/ère	bitter
amer d'aloès	bitter aloes
americaine	with tomatoes, onions, wine, herbs and crayfish or lobster tails
américain, pouding	pounded and sieved plum pudding
américaine, salade	tomatoes, hard-boiled eggs, celeriac
américaine, sauce	a seafood sauce, enriched with butter
amiral	with shellfish and mushrooms
ammocète	eel-like fish found in the Seine
amou	a cheese made in Béarn
amourettes	marrowbone
amsdem	a pink-fleshed peach with delicate flavour
amuse-gueule	cocktail snack
amusettes	appetiser, cocktail snack
ananas	pineapple
anchoïade	anchovy paste; pounded anchovies
anchois	anchovy
anchois, beurre d'	anchovy butter
anchois, pâté d'	anchovy paste
ancholade	anchovy-flavoured toast

ancienne	with braised onions and mushrooms; with forcemeat balls of chicken and truffles; with duchesse potatoes and diced kidneys
andalouse	with tomatoes, sweet peppers, chipolatas
andalouse, fruits	assorted poached fruits
andalouse, salade	spiced rice, sweet peppers and tomatoes
andalouse, sauce	with tomato purée, sweet peppers and parsley
andouilles	chitterlings, sausages made from pork offal
andouillettes	small chitterling sausages
âne, poivre d'	cows' milk cheese from the Riviera
aneth	dill
ange de mer, angel or angelot	angel-fish; monk-fish
angélique	angelica
anglaise	egg and breadcrumbed prior to frying; with caper sauce; with mixed vegetables
anglaise, crème	light egg custard
anglais, pouding	suet pudding with raisins and fruits
anguille	eel
anguille de mer	conger eel
anguilles en vert	eels cooked in white wine and herbs
anguries	watermelon salad
anis	anise, aniseed
anisette	liqueur based on aniseed
anis vert	aniseed, sweet cumin
anna, pommes	sliced casseroled potatoes
annette, pommes	matchstick-cut casseroled potatoes
anodonte	a freshwater mollusc similar to mussels
anon	Breton name for haddock
anversoise	with hop shoots and potatoes
apéritif	a drink taken before a meal
aphie	onos, rockling, whiting-like fish
apogen	cardinal fish: variety of red mullet
appareil	mixture used for stuffing
appareil Maintenon	mixture of soubise and béchamel

	sauces with mushrooms
appareil Matignon	sliced vegetables diluted with madeira
appareil Tvarogue	cream cheese and butter mixture
appétissant	appetising, tasty
appétit	appetite
arachide	peanut, groundnut
arachide, beurre d'	peanut butter
arachide, huile d'	peanut oil
araignée or **araignée de mer**	spider-crab
arapède	an edible limpet or barnacle
arbenne	snow partridge
arbre	tree
arca	mollusc similar to a mussel
arcanette	name for teal in Lorraine
arch	mollusc similar to mussel
archiduc	with paprika and cream
ardennaise	usually cooked en cocotte with juniper berries
aremberg, pouding	a kirsch-flavoured bavarois with fruits
argenteuil	with asparagus
argenteuil, salade	potatoes, asparagus tips, chervil, hard-boiled eggs
ariégeoise	with green cabbage and pickled pork and sometimes with kidney beans
ariégeoise, soupe	with root vegetables, salt pork, garlic and confit of goose
arlésienne	with aubergines or chicory hearts and tomatoes
armagnac	a gentle brandy
armenonville	with anna potatoes and morels; with artichoke hearts, tomatoes and french beans
armoricaine	in the fashion of Brittany; with a lobster and cream sauce; a choice variety of oyster; piquant sauce of wine, brandy, garlic, shallots, tomatoes
aromate	spice; aromatic
aromatique	aromatic
arôme	aroma; flavour

arrigny	a winter cheese made in Champagne
arroche	orach, a spinach-like vegetable
artagnan	with mushrooms, tomatoes, croquette potatoes
artichaut	artichoke
artichauts barigoule	stuffed, braised artichokes
artichauts Clamart	young fried artichokes with peas and lettuce
artichauts, coeurs d'	artichoke hearts
artichauts, fonds d'	artichoke bases
artichauts, moelle d'	artichoke stalks
asco	a Corsican cheese
asperges	asparagus
asperges à la flamande	hot asparagus with melted butter and eggs
asperges à la fontenelle	hot asparagus dipped in soft-boiled eggs
asperges, pointes d'	asparagus tips
assaisonné	seasoned with
assiette(é)	plate, plateful, plated
assiette anglaise	plate of assorted cold meats
assiette campagnarde	dish of assorted local foods
assiette scandinave	dish of assorted fish
assiette volante	plate of varied items
athénienne	with tomatoes, onions, peppers, aubergines
athérine	sand-smelt, small fish with flesh similar to bass
atoca	cranberry
attereaux	kebabs
aubergine	egg-plant
aublet	small river fish of the carp family
aubourg	dace, a freshwater fish
Auge, Vallée d'	with Calvados, apples and cream
aulx	garlic (plural of ail)
aumonière	pancake
auriol	local name for mackerel in Marseilles
aurore, sauce	pink sauce containing tomato purée
autrichienne	with paprika; with onion, fennel and cream

autruche	ostrich
autun	a cow's milk cheese
aveline	hazelnut, filbert nut
avocat	avocado pear
avocette	avocet, small wading bird
avoine	oats
avoine, soupe bouillie d'	oatmeal porridge
Aydes	an Orléanais cheese
aythya	pochard, species of wild duck

baba or baba au rhum	small yeast cake soaked in rum or other spirit
babeurre	buttermilk
babeurre, soupe de	buttermilk soup
bacile	samphire, a sea plant
badianne	a strong, aniseed flavoured spirit
badoise	with red cabbage, lean bacon and creamed potatoes; with stoned cherries
Badoit	a sparkling spa water from Evian
bagatelle, salade	with carrots, mushrooms, asparagus tips
bagnation, salade	with artichoke hearts, celeriac, macaroni, truffles and tongue
baguette	a long thin loaf
baie	berry
baie du sureau	elderberry
baigné	lying in, soaked with
baisers	tiny meringues sandwiched with cream
bajoues	cheeks, chaps (of pig)
bakeofe	type of Alsation hotpot
balane	acorn barnacle
baliste	triggerfish, a delicate fish prepared like tuna
ballotin	terrine, rough pâté
ballotine	boned, stuffed and braised shoulder
bamboche	bamboo shoot
banane	banana
banane au four	baked banana
banane beauharnais	banana with rum and macaroons
banon	a small goat cheese from Provence

banquière	with quenelles, mushrooms and truffles
banquière, sauce	a rich sauce made with madeira wine
bar	sea perch: dace; bass
barbadine	passion-fruit
barbarie	Barbary duck
barbarin	fish of the mullet family
barbe-de-capucin	wild chicory
barbe-de-chèvre	a type of tough mushroom
barbe-de-bouc	wild salsify
barbeau	barbel, river fish
barberon	southern French name for salsify
barbillon	barbel, a river fish
barbot(e) or barbotte	barbot: eel pout; freshwater fish
barboteur	common name for the domestic duck
barbotine	tansy; mugwort
barbouche	couscous with tripe
barbue	brill, a flat sea-fish
barde	a slice of bacon
barigoule	a very tasty mushroom
Bar-le-Duc	red and white currant preserves
barquette	oval or boat-shaped tartlet shell
bartavelle	rock partridge; red-legged partridge
baselle	indian spinach
basilic	basil
basquaise	with tomatoes, garlic, sweet peppers; with mushrooms, raw ham, anna potatoes
basque, gâteau	tart made with almond paste and jam
bassin	edible limpet/barnacle
bat	tail of fish
bâtarde, sauce	egg, lemon and butter sauce
batelière	with mushrooms, onions, eggs, crayfish
bâton	a long thin French loaf
bâtonnets	preparations in tiny stick shapes
bâtonnets de crabe	crabsticks
bâtons	preparations in tiny stick shapes
battu	beaten, flattened
baudroie	monkfish
bavarois	a fruit-flavoured custard cream dessert
bavaroise, sauce	a piquant egg and cream sauce with

	crayfish tails
bavette	a beef steak, skirt of beef
Bayonne, jambon de	raw ham, speciality of Bayonne
béarnaise, sauce	egg yolk, white wine and tarragon sauce
béatilles	sweetbreads, cocks' combs, liver and kidneys
Béatrix	with morels, carrots, artichokes
Beaucaire, salade	with celery, ham, chicken, apples, herbs and beetroot
beaufort	cheese from the Alps region
beauharnais	with artichoke hearts and potato balls
beaumont	gruyère-type cheese from the Alps
beaupré de Roybon	a cheese
beauvilliers	with spinach balls
bécasse	woodcock
bécasseau	young woodcock
bécassin	great snipe
bécassine	snipe
beccabunga	a European cress
becfigue or bec-fin	small, lark-like bird
béchamel sauce	a classic white cream sauce
bêche-de-mer	sea cucumber
beckenoffe	a mutton, pork and potato stew, from Alsace region
béguinette	a garden warbler, small edible bird
beigne	doughnut
beignet	fritter
belle-alliance	type of pear
belle angevine	an enormous pear with little flavour
belle-chevreuse	type of peach
belle-de-berry	type of pear
belle-de-Fontenay	type of raspberry
belle-et-bonne	type of pear
belle-garde	type of peach
belle Hélène	served with ice cream and hot chocolate sauce; with mushrooms, peas, carrots, croquette potatoes
bellone	type of fig
belon	type of flat oyster
Bénédictine	a liqueur made in Fécamp

bénédictine	with salt cod and truffles
bénédictine, oeufs	poached eggs cooked with cream and Benedictine served on a bed of salt cod or bread croûtons
bèquefigue	small, lark-like bird
Bercy	with wine, bone marrow and shallots
bercy, sauce	a fish stock sauce with butter and parsley
berdanel	variety of edible fungus
bergamote	very fragrant, long-keeping pear; bergamot
bergues	a cheese from Flanders
berle	water parsnip (leaves are edible; roots poisonous)
berlingot	caramel: a peppermint candy
bernacle	edible limpet/barnacle
Bernard l'ermite	hermit crab
bernique	edible limpet
berny	with lentil purée and truffles
berrichonne	with cabbage, chestnuts, onions, bacon
béryx	a firm-fleshed fish
besi	salted and dried cow's meat; variety of pear
bête	beast; bird
bête rousse	6 months to year-old wild boar
bête de compagnie	1–2 year old wild boar
bette	swiss chard, seakale beet
betterave	beetroot
betterave à sucre	sugar beet
beugnon	a Burgundian cheese
beurre	butter
beurre bercy	butter with shallots and bone marrow
beurre blanc	cooked flavoured butter; sauce of shallots in white wine with whipped-in butter
beurre d'anchois	anchovy butter
beurré d'Angleterre	a variety of pear
beurre d'arachide	peanut butter
beurré d'Aremberg	gritty type of pear
beurre de cacao	cocoa butter

beurre de coco	coconut butter
beurré diel	gritty type of pear
beurre du lait	dairy butter
beurre gascon	rendered duck fat with shallots and wine
beurré Giffard	early variety of pear
beurré Hardy	delicately-flavoured late pear
beurre maître d'hôtel	butter with parsley, lemon juice, salt and pepper
beurre noir	browned butter
beursaudes	pork greaves
biarotte	with mushrooms and duchesse potatoes
bichiques	tiny fish
bien cuit	well cooked
bière	beer
bière blonde	pale ale
bière de gingembre	ginger-beer
bière sous pression	draught beer
biftek, bifteck	beefsteak
bigarade	Seville orange, bitter oranges
bigarade, sauce	brown sauce with bitter oranges
bigarde	bitter or Seville orange
bigarreau	cherry
bigorneau	winkle
bijane	a cold soup containing bread soaked in red wine
Billy By	mussel soup
bis	wholemeal, wholewheat
biscotin	potato crisp, ship's biscuit
biscotte	rusk
biscuit	biscuit
biscuit à cuiller	sponge finger
biscuit de Savoie	sponge cake
biset	wild pigeon
bisque	thick, creamy shellfish soup
bissale	patisserie made from buttered bread dough
bitok	type of beef rissole
Bizet	with savoury tapioca and chicken

bizontine	with potato, cauliflower and lettuce
blanc/blanche	white
blanc d'oeuf	egg-white
blanchailles	whitebait: young herrings
blanquet	a variety of pear
blanquette	meat or poultry cooked in white wine and cream
blavet	russula, a variety of edible fungus
blé	wheat
blé de sarrasin	buckwheat
blé noir	buckwheat
blennie cagnette	blenny, a freshwater fish
blète or blette	swiss chard, spinach beet
bleu	blue; blue cheese
bleu	(of meat) underdone
bleu, au	very quick method of cooking fish
bleu d'Auvergne	a blue cheese made from both goats' and cows' milk
bleu de Basillac	a blue sheeps' milk cheese from Limousin
bleu de Bresse	creamy blue cheese from the French Alps
bleu de Corse	a Corsican blue cheese
bleu de Quercy	blue cheese from the Dordogne
blinis	small, thick pancakes
boeuf	beef
boeuf à la mode	beef with vegetables braised in red wine
boeuf bouilli	boiled beef
boeuf bourguignonne	beef cooked in red wine
boeuf de conserve	corned beef
boeuf salé	salt beef
bogue	boops, a Mediterranean fish
bohémienne	with rice, tomatoes and onions
bohémienne, sauce	an enriched white sauce eaten cold
boisson	drink
boitelle	with minced mushrooms
bolée	bowlful
bombe	ice cream in bomb shape
bon	good

bon appétit	enjoy your meal!
bon bon	sweet; candy
Bon-Chrétien	variety of pear
bondon	a whole-milk, loaf-shaped Normandy cheese
bon-henri	wild spinach
bonne femme	for meat: with potatoes, onions and bacon
	for fish: poached in white wine with mushrooms
boops	fish similar to sea-bream
bordelaise	with wine, shallots and beef marrow; with mushrooms; with artichokes and potatoes
bordelaise, sauce	with beef marrow, parsley and red wine
bordet vert	type of edible mushroom
bordure	dish in the shape of a crown or ring
bortsch	Russian beetroot soup
bosson macéré	a Provençal winter cheese
botargo	made from the roe of grey mullet
botte d'asperges	bunch of asparagus
bottereaux de hangon	a deep-fried fritter
bouc	regional name for shrimp (Aunis)
boucan	smoked meat
bouchée	mouthful, cocktail nibble
bouchée à la reine	chicken filled vol-au-vent with mushroom sauce
boudin	large fat sausage
boudin blanc	white sausage made with milk and chicken
boudin de volaille	large sausage made with chicken forcemeat
boudin noir	black pudding, blood sausage
boudin sucré	black or white pudding with sultanas
bouffi	smoked herring, kippers
bougras	vegetable soup from Périgord
bouillabaisse	a fish soup or stew from Provence
bouillade	a wine sauce used for cooking snails or fish
bouillant(e)	boiling

bouilleture	fish stew, mainly eel, from Anjou
bouilli	boiled
bouillie	gruel; porridge; hasty-pudding
bouillinade	fish and potato pie
bouilliture	eel soup
bouillon	broth; stock
boulangère	with potatoes and onions
boule de neige	ball-shaped ice or sponge covered with cream
boule de trille	a Normandy cheese
boulette	fish or meat ball
boulette d'Avesnes	a strong smelling soft cheese made in Flanders
boulette de Cambrai	a mild, herb-flavoured cheese made in Cambrai
bouquet	prawn
bouquet garni	bunch of herbs
bouquetière	with mixed vegetable garnish
bourbotte	burbot, a freshwater fish
bourcette	lambs' lettuce, corn salad
bourdaloue	whole fruit in a pastry case; dessert with apricots, semolina, kirsch and macaroons
bourdelot	whole apple turnover in pastry case
bourgeoise	with carrots, onions and lean bacon
bourguignon(ne)	made with red wine, onions and mushrooms
bourigoule	a very well-flavoured mushroom
bourrache	borage
bourride	a fish soup or stew from Provence
bourriols	buckwheat pancakes
bourse-à-berger, also bourse-à-pasteur and boursette	lambs' lettuce, corn salad
brabançonne	with endive and potato croquettes; with Brussels sprouts and mornay sauce
bragance	with stuffed tomatoes and potato croquettes
braisé	braised
brancas	individual anna potatoes

brancas, sauce	veal-flavoured sauce
brandade de morue	salt cod pounded with garlic, oil and cream; a salt-cod fish pie
brasillé	grilled, broiled
brebis	flesh of a young ewe
bréhan	with artichoke hearts, cauliflower, broad bean purée
bréjauda, soupe	with cabbage and bacon
brelins	name given to winkles in Normandy
brème	freshwater bream
brème de mer	pomfret; sea bream
brési	sliced dried beef
brésilien, pouding	moulded tapioca pudding
bresolles	dish of layered sliced and minced meats
bressane, salade	with lettuce, chicken, truffles, asparagus tips
Bresse, bleu de	a blue cheese
bretonneau	turbot
bretonne	with haricot beans; with leeks, mushrooms and onions
bretzel	pretzel, salted cocktail biscuit
breuvage	beverage, drink
briançon	a cheese from Dauphiné
brie	a soft, fermented cheese
brignole	a kind of dried plum
brigoule	a tasty mushroom
Brillat	a mild, creamy cheese from Normandy
Brillat-Savarin	with foie gras, truffles, duchesse potatoes; a cheese made in Normandy
brimont, salade	with artichoke hearts, crayfish tails, olives, truffles and eggs in curry-flavoured mayonnaise
brioche	slightly sweetened bread roll
brioli	Corsican dessert made with chestnut flour
brionne	custard marrow
Bristol	with rice croquettes and flageolet beans
broccana	sausage-meat and veal pâté

broccio	a Corsican goats' or ewes'-milk cheese
broche, à la	spit-roasted
brochet	pike
brocheton	pickerel, baby pike
brochette	kebab, skewer
brocoli	broccoli
brouet	thin gruel
brouillade	stewed in oil
brouillé	scrambled
brousse	a goats' cheese from Provence
brousses	a ewes'-milk cheese from the Riviera
broutard	3 to 4 month old kid
broutes or broutons	cabbage shoots
brugnon	nectarine
brûlé	burnt, toasted
brûlée, crème	a caramel custard dessert
brûlot	sugar-lump soaked in brandy and flamed over a cup of coffee
brunoise	mixed diced or shredded vegetables added to soup
bruxelles, choux de	Brussels sprouts
bruxelloise	with sprouts, potatoes and chicory
bucarde	cockle
buccins	whelks
bûche	Swiss roll
bûche de Noël	Christmas log cake
bugne	a fritter
buisson	special dish
bulots	whelks
burbot	a freshwater fish
butteaux	a Burgundian cheese
byrrh	a wine-based apéritif

cabécou	a small goat cheese from Dordogne
cabillaud	cod
cabinet, pouding	a custard-soaked sponge dessert
cabiros	kid, young goat
cabliaud	cod
cabot	chub, a freshwater fish
cabri(s)	a kid, young goat
cabrion	a cone-shaped goat cheese
cacao	cocoa
cachat	a ewes'-milk cheese ripened with vinegar
café	coffee
café au lait	coffee with milk
café complet	continental breakfast
café express	expresso coffee
café filtre	filtered coffee
café, grain de	coffee bean
café liégeoise	hot coffee poured over ice cream
caféine	caffeine
café noir	black coffee
cagouille	type of snail
caieu	giant mussel
caille	quail
caillé	curds, curdled milk
caillebotte	curds
caillebotte chardonette	a cheese from Saumur
caillettes	faggots
cailletot	Normandy name for young turbot

caillette	rennet; a coarse sausage of pig's liver and herbs
caillette de brebis	a sausage of sheep's liver and offal
caisse, en	in cases, wrapped with pastry, etc.
cake	fruit cake
calamar	squid, inkfish
calappe	a crustacean similar to the crab
calisson	small, iced almond cake
calmar	squid, inkfish
calvados	apple brandy
calvilles	type of apple
camard	gurnard, a sea fish
Cambridge, sauce	cold, spicy sauce with anchovies, herbs and English mustard
camembert	a soft fermented cheese
camérani	with foie gras and truffles
camomille, thé de	camomile tea
campagnarde	in country style
camus de Bretagne	variety of globe artichoke
canapé	small cocktail savoury
canard	duck
canard d'Inde	Barbary duck
canardeau	duckling
canard sauvage	wild duck
canard siffleur	widgeon
canaron	gurnard, a sea fish
cancaillotte	a very strong, high-flavoured cheese from Jura
cancalaise	with assorted mushrooms; with oysters and shrimps
cancale	a plump, white oyster
cancalaise, salade	with potatoes, oysters, truffles
canepetière	small bustard, bird of duck family
caneton	duckling
caneton rouennaise	duckling cooked with wine and brandy
canette	female duckling
cangalaise	with oysters and shrimps
canneberge	cranberry
cannelle	cinnamon
canneloni(s)	canneloni, savoury filled pasta tubes

cantal	hard, strong cheese from Auvergne
cantaloup	cantaloupe melon
capel or capelan	small fish similar to whiting
capendu	variety of red apple
capilotade	reheated poultry stew; small pieces
capitaine	sea fish similar to carp
capoum	rascasse, scorpion fish
câpre	caper
câpres de capucine	nasturtium seeds
caprice, salade	with tongue, ham, truffles, artichoke hearts
capucin	hunter's name for hare
capucine	nasturtium
caqhuse	a fresh piece of braised pork
carafe or carafon	jug, pitcher
caramel	caramel, burnt sugar
caramel au beurre	butterscotch, toffee
caramel, crème	a baked custard dessert with caramel
caramelisé	caramelised, with burnt sugar
carbonnade	beef stew with beer, onions and herbs
cardamome	cardamon
cardeau	regional name for sardine
cardinal	with shellfish, truffles and mushrooms
cardinal, sauce	rich red fish sauce with truffles and lobster butter
cardine	small white fish
cardon	cardoon, vegetable of artichoke family
cargolade	snails cooked in wine
cari	curry
carignan, fruits	mixed poached soft fruits
caringue	long fish similar to mackerel
Carmen, salade	with red peppers, chicken, peas and rice
carolines	small éclairs served as hors d'oeuvres
carotte	carrot
caroube	carob bean
carpe	carp, freshwater fish
carpeau or carpillon	very small carp
carpion	variety of trout
carré d'agneau	rack or loin of lamb

carré de Bonneville	a cheese from Normandy
carré de l'Est	a mildly rich cheese from Normandy
carré de porc	loin of pork
carrelet	plaice, flounder
cartouches, poires	whole pears baked in pastry case
carvi	caraway
carvi, grains de	caraway seeds
caseum	coagulated casein, a fresh cheese
cassate or cassete	Neapolitan ice-cream
casse-croûte	a snack
casserole	stew; a rice dish in timbale shape
cassette d'Auvergne	leg of lamb with lentils and braised cabbage
cassis	blackcurrant; a blackcurrant liqueur
cassolette	thick soup or stew
cassoulet	a stew of various meats always with beans
cassonade	brown sugar
castiglione	with mushrooms, ham, risotto and aubergines
castillane	with tomatoes, onions, croquette potatoes
catalane	with aubergines and/or artichoke hearts
catigau d'anguilles	an eel stew from Provence
catillac	variety of pear which turns red when cooked
cavaillon	melon from Cavaillon with orange-coloured flesh
caviare	sturgeons' roe
cavour	with mushrooms and chicken livers
cayenne, poivre de	cayenne pepper
cayuga	a large black duck
cédrat	variety of lemon
cédrat, pâté de	a citron preserve from Bayonne
céleri	celery
céleri-ravé	celeriac, celery roots
célestine	thin soup garnished with strips of pancake
cendré de la brie	a cheese from L'Île de France
cendres, sous les	cooked in the cinders

cendrillon, salade	with celeriac, truffles, artichoke hearts, apples and asparagus tips
cèpe	large, rich mushroom
céréale	cereal
cerf	venison
cerfeuil	chervil
cerise	cherry
cerises à l'allemande	morello cherries preserved in vinegar
cermont, pouding	a rum and chestnut-flavoured bavarois
cerneau	green walnut
cervelas	saveloy, large sausage usually made from pork
cervelles	brains
cévenole	with chestnuts, onions and bacon
chabichou	a soft, sweet goat cheese
chabissous	little cheese made from goats' or ewes' milk
chaboisseau	a Mediterranean fish used in bouillabaisse
chabot	chub, a delicate freshwater fish
chabrol	glass of red wine added to the last few spoonfuls of soup in the dish
chaigny	a cheese produced in Orléans
chair	flesh, meat
chair à saucisse	sausagemeat
chalonnaise	with cockerel kidney tartlets
chambertin	red wine sauce made with Chambertin wine
chambord	with fish quenelles and soft roes; cooked in red wine
chambord, sauce	a red wine and fish stock sauce
chamoure	a type of marrow flan
champenois	of the Champagne region; a cheese from the Champagne area
champignon	mushroom
champigny	a type of jam turnover, a patisserie
champoléon	a cheese from Dauphiné
chanoinesse	carrots in cream with truffles
chanterelle	an edible, pinkish mushroom
chantilly	with or containing whipped cream

chantilly crème	cream whipped up with caster sugar and vanilla
chaource	a soft cream cheese made in the Champagne area
chapeau	pie-crust; vol-au-vent lid
chapelure	brown breadcrumbs (for frying)
chapelure, sauce	bread sauce
chapon	capon
chapon à l'ail	uncooked garlic bread with oil and vinegar
chapon de mer	scorpion fish
charbon	charcoal
charbonnier	coal-fish, a type of cod
charcuterie	cold meats
charcutière, sauce	thick brown onion and wine sauce
charlotte	a moulded sponge and bavarois dessert which is eaten hot or cold
charolais	a dry goat cheese from Burgundy
charollais	beef from the Charollais herd of Burgundy
charollaise	with turnip purée and cauliflower
Chartres	with fondant potatoes and tarragon; with mushrooms and braised lettuce; with new turnips, pea purée and mashed potatoes
chartreuse	a herbal liqueur (may be green or yellow); a dish prepared in a mould and turned out when served
chartreuse de légumes	a layered vegetable mould sealed with forcemeat
chasselas	a variety of grape
chasseur	with mushrooms, shallots and white wine
chasseur, sauce	with mushrooms, shallots and tomatoes
châtaigne	sweet chestnut
chateaubriand	a thick, double-fillet steak
château, entrecôte	porterhouse steak
château, pommes	roasted potatoes
châtelaine	with artichokes and chestnut purée

chatteries	delicacies, dainties
chaud(e)	hot, warm
chaudée	an apple tart from Lorraine
chaud-froid	cold and jellied (usually chicken)
chaud-froid blanche	a rich cold velouté sauce made with madeira
chaud-froid brúne	a cold jellied sauce made with madeira wine
chaud-froid poisson	a cold jellied fish dish
chaud-froid volaille	a cold jellied poultry dish
chaudrée	thick fish soup or stew from Charente
chaudronne	casserole
chauffé	warmed, heated
chaumont	a cheese made in the Champagne region
chausson	a puff pastry turnover, usually with fruit
chavanne	freshwater chub
chayotte	custard marrow
chemise, en	wrapped in pastry
chemitré	a type of waffle
chèque-repas	luncheon voucher
chester	French name for Cheshire cheese
chevaine	chub, a freshwater fish
cheval	horse
cheval, pieds de	very large oysters
chevaline	of a horse
chevesne	chub, a freshwater fish
chèvre	goat; goat's milk cheese
chevreau	kid, young goat
chevret	a goat cheese from Bresse
chevrette	a cheese from the Savoy area; young roebuck; a shrimp, prawn
chevreuil	venison, roebuck
chevreuse	with chervil
chevreuse	with artichoke hearts, truffles and noisette potatoes
chevreuse, pouding	a semolina pudding with fruits and liqueurs
chevrier	a green haricot bean

chevrotins	goat cheese from Savoy
chevrotton de Mâcon	a cone-shaped goat cheese from Mâcon
Chicago, salade	with tomatoes, asparagus, french beans, foie gras
chich	kebab
chiche	chickpea
chicolle	peaches in red wine with toast
chicon	chicory
chicorée	endive
chicorée frisée	curly endive
chien de mer	dog-fish, salmon-like sea fish
chiffonade	cut into fine strips or ribbons for garnish
chinchard	a fish resembling a mackerel
chinois	small green orange preserved in brandy; a spicy yeast-cake with cinnamon and raisins
chinonaise	cabbage leaves stuffed with sausage-meat
chipirone	squid
chipirons à l'encre	squid stewed in its own ink
chipolata	chipolata sausage; garnished with sausage, onions and chestnuts
chips	potato crisps
Chivry, sauce	with shallots, white wine and butter
chlorophyll	mint-flavoured (usually of desserts)
chocolat	chocolate
chocolat à croquer	dessert chocolate
choesels	a Belgian stew of tripe and sweetbreads
choisy	with braised lettuce and château potatoes
choix, au	to your choice
choron	with artichoke hearts, peas, noisette potatoes
choron, sauce	a white egg and wine sauce with tomato purée
choten	pigs' cheeks
chou	cabbage
choucroute	sauerkraut, pickled cabbage

chou de Chine	Chinese leaves
chou de mer	sea kale
chou de Milan	Savoy cabbage
chouée	boiled, buttered green cabbage
choufleur	cauliflower
chou frisé	kale
chou marin	sea kale
chou, pâté à	choux pastry
chou pommé	garden cabbage; white-heart cabbage
chou-rave	kohl-rabi
chou rouge	red cabbage
chou vert	green garden cabbage
choux à la crème	éclair, cream bun
choux au fromage	cheese puffs
choux de Bruxelles	Brussels sprouts
chouzé	a cheese from Saumur
christes-marines	samphire
ciboule	spring onion, scallion
ciboulettes	chives
cidre	cider
cidre bouchée	bottled cider
cierp de Luchon	a cheese made in the Comté de Foix
cimier	haunch, rump
cinq	five
citeaux	a Burgundian cheese
citron	lemon
citron, écorcée de	lemon peel
citron, essence de	lemon oil
citronnade	still lemon drink
citron pressé	drink of lemon juice
citron vert	lime
citrouille	pumpkin
cive	green onion
civelle	young eel
civet	rich stew, usually of furred game
civet de langouste	spiny lobster stew
civet de lièvre	jugged hare
civette	chives
clafoutis	a batter cake or pudding with fruit

claires, fines de	type of small oyster
clairette	lambs' lettuce; a light sparkling wine
Clamart	with artichoke hearts, peas and potatoes
Clamart, purée	purée of green peas
clavaire	a tough mushroom
clayère	oyster bed/park
Clermont	with chestnuts and onions; with stuffed cabbage rolls
clochard	variety of apple
clos, or clou, de girofle	clove
clovisse	clam
coagulé	curdled, soured
cocagne	feast, treat
cochenille	cochineal
cochevis	crested lark, small edible bird
cochon	pig, pork
cochonailles	pork products
cochon de lait	sucking pig
cochon, fromage de	brawn
coco, noix de	coconut
coco, lait de	coconut milk
cocotte, en	in a casserole, stewed
coeur	heart; white cream cheese
coeur à la crème	moulded crème fraîche and egg whites
coeurs d'Arras	thin chocolate biscuits; a creamy cheese from Arras
coeurs d'artichauts	artichoke hearts
coeurs de palmiers	palm hearts
cognac	brandy
cognac trois étoiles	three-star brandy
cognassier	quince-tree
coing	quince
Colbert	fried breadcrumbed fish
Colbert, fruits	fruits poached in vanilla syrup
Colbert, sauce	rich sauce made with madeira wine
colin	hake, green pollack
collet de mouton	neck/scrag end of mutton
collioure, sauce	mayonnaise with purée of anchovies and herbs

collop	escalope, slice of meat or fish
Colnet, consommé	thin chicken soup with threaded eggs
colombe	dove
Colonel, sorbet	lemon water-ice with vodka
col vert	type of wild duck
colza, huile de	rapeseed oil
comestibles	foodstuffs
commodore	with crayfish tails, mussels and fish dumplings
commodore, consommé	thin fish soup garnished with clams
compôte	mixture, in jellied mould
compôte composée	macédoine of mixed poached fruits
compôte de fruits	poached or stewed fruits
comté	a Jura cheese similar to Gruyère
concoilotte	a cheese made in Franche-Comté
concombre	cucumber
concorde	with peas, glazed carrots and potatoes
condé	usually with rice
condé, purée	purée of red beans
confiserie	confectionery, preserves
confit	fruit or vegetables preserved in sugar, brandy or vinegar; meat cooked and preserved in its own fat
confit d'oie	preserved goose
confiture	jam
confiture d'oranges	marmalade
confiture, tartine à la	slice of bread and jam
congre	conger eel
conserves alimentaires	preserved/tinned foods
conserves au vinaigre	pickles
conserves en boîte	tinned foods
consommation	drink
consommé	clear soup; stock; beef tea
Conti, or Conty	with lentils, bacon and possibly potatoes
contrefilet	rib/T-bone/Porterhouse steak
Contrex/Contrexéville	a still spa water
copeaux	shavings, grated
coppa	a highly-flavoured Corsican sausage

coprin	edible mushroom
coq	cockerel, chicken
coq au vin	cockerel cooked in red wine
coq d'inde	turkey cock
coq de bruyère	capercailzie, wood grouse
coq faisan	cock pheasant
coq rayé	clam, prairie oyster
coque	shell (of nut, egg, etc); cockle
coque, à la	boiled egg; soft-boiled
coque du Lot	an Easter cake made in the region of Lot
coquelet	baby chicken
coque, oeuf à la	soft-boiled egg
coqueret	edible strawberry-tomato
coquibus, lapin	jointed rabbit, casseroled with onions and bacon
coquillages	shellfish
coquille	shell, shell-shaped container
coquille, huîtres à la	scalloped oysters
coquilles St. Jacques	scallops
coquillettes	pasta shells
corbeau	crow, rook
corbeille	basket
coriandre	coriander
corneille	crow, rook, jackdaw
cornel	a pickled reddish cherry type of fruit
cornet	cornet, pastry horn
cornet de glace	cone shaped ice-cream
cornet de pâtisserie	cream horn
cornichon	gherkin
cornouille	a pickled reddish cherry type fruit
corossoe	custard-apple
Corse, bleu de	a blue cheese from the Riviera
cosse	pod, husk, hull
côte	chop, cutlet
côte de boeuf	rib of beef
côtelette	chop, cutlet
cotignac	quince marmalade/jelly
cotriade	seafish stew from Brittany

cou	neck
cou d'oie	goose-neck
coucou	cuckoo
coucoumelle	grisette, edible mushroom
coucouzelle	courgette, zucchini
couenne	pork rind, crackling
coulemelle	parasol mushroom
coulibiac	a hot fish pie/turnover
coulibiac de poulet	a hot chicken pie/turnover
coulis	sauce, liquid purée
coulommiers	a soft cream cheese, a type of Brie
coupe glacée	sundae, ice-cream dessert
coupe Jacques	fruit soaked in liqueur served with ice cream
courge	gourd, pumpkin, marrow
courge citrouille	pumpkin
courgeron	courgette
courgette	baby marrow
couronne	crown-shaped, a ring
court bouillon	specially prepared cooking liquor; dish with a wine sauce
couscous	African dish of millet flour and meats
cousinat	a rich chestnut soup
cousinette	soup made from spinach, sorrel, lettuce and herbs
couteau	razor-fish
covenne	pork rind, crackling
crabe	crab
crameou	type of shell-less crab
crapaudine	way of preparing fowl, especially pigeon
craquelin	a crunchy cake; a cracknel biscuit
craquelot	bloater
craquelot de Dunkirk	herring smoked in hazelnut tree leaves
crassane	variety of pear
Crécy	usually with carrots
crème	cream; with cream
crème anglaise	custard sauce made with eggs
crème bordelaise	prune and cream purée

crème caprice	meringue and cream purée
crème caramel	baked custard with caramel sauce
crème Chantilly	thick whipped cream
crème des Vosges	a soft cream cheese from Alsace
crème fouettée	whipped cream
crème fraîche	slightly soured cream
crème frangipane	type of vanilla pastry cream
crème, fromage à la	cream cheese
crème Mont Blanc	chestnut and cream purée
crème renversée	a cold custard cream dessert
crémet	cream cheese, often made from goats' milk
crémeux	creamy
créole	usually with rice and sweet peppers
créole	dessert with fruit and rice
crêpe	pancake
crêpes dentelles	very light pancakes filled and rolled into cigar shapes
crêpes fourrées	stuffed pancakes
crêpes suzettes	thin pancakes in orange sauce
crépinette	small sausage encased in a caul
cresson	watercress
cresson de fontaine	watercress
cressonière, salade	with watercress and potato
crête de coq	cockscomb
creuse	long oyster
crevettes	shrimps, prawns
crevettes grises	shrimps
crevettes roses	prawns
cristallisé	crystallized
cristallisé, sucre	granulated sugar
croissant	crescent shaped roll made from flaky pastry
cromesquis	deep fried meat balls
croncel	large, delicately-flavoured peach
croquant	crisp, crunchy; petit four
croque au sel	raw, served with salt
croquembouche	a tasty mouthful
croque-monsieur	toasted sandwich with ham and cheese
croquet	hard almond biscuit; snap; parkin

croquette	rissole; ball-shaped item, sweet or savoury
croquettes, pommes	creamed potatoes, rolled into sausage shapes, egged and breadcrumbed and fried
croquignolle	type of meringue biscuit
crosnes du Japon	Japanese artichokes (white-fleshed root vegetables)
crotte de chocolat	a chocolate
crottin	strongly-flavoured goat cheese
crottin de Chavignol	semi-hard goat cheese
croustade	pastry shell, covering
croustadines	tiny shapes of puff pastry
croustillant	crusty, crisp
croûte	cheese rind; crust of pie or bread
croûte, en	in a pastry case
croûtons	small fried bread cubes as soup garnish
crû	raw
crudités	raw vegetables served as hors d'oeuvre
crustaces	shellfish
crû, vin de	local wine
cuiller or cuillère	spoon
cuire	to cook
cuire à l'eau	to boil
cuire au four	to bake, roast
cuisse de poulet	chicken leg
cuisses	thighs
cuisses de grenouilles	frogs' legs
cuisson	stock; cooking liquid
cuissot	haunch
cuit	cooked
cuit à point	medium cooked
cuit, bien	well cooked
cul-blanc	white-tailed great snipe
cul de veau	haunch of veal
cullis	shrimp soup
culotte de boeuf	rump of beef; aitchbone
Cumberland, sauce	sauce with redcurrant jelly, shallots, port, mustard, ginger and fruit juices
curaçao	liqueur made from Seville oranges

currie   curry
Cussy   with artichoke hearts, mushrooms,
                        cocks' kidneys; with chestnut purée,
                        truffles and mushrooms

Dalila, salade	with bananas, apples and celery
Dame-Blanche	ice-cream with poached peaches and pineapple; also chicken consommé
Dame-Blanche, fruits	poached peaches on ice cream
dard	dace, a freshwater fish
darne	slice, slab, steak (of salmon etc.)
dartois	puff pastry patisserie with almonds; tiny sweet or savoury hors d'oeuvres; with carrots, turnips and celery
datte	date
datte fourrée	stuffed date
daube, en	stewed with wine and herbs
daubière	a stewpan, casserole
daumont	with soft roes, mushrooms, crayfish tails
dauphin	a cheese made in northern France
dauphine, pommes	of potatoes: a deep-fried *duchesse* mixture with choux-paste
dauphinois, gratin	sliced potatoes cooked with cream
dauphinoise, salade	salad with tomato, nuts, oranges and crab
daurade	sea bream
décaféiné	decaffeinated
déchlorure	salt-free
decize	a brie-like Nivernais cheese
découpé	carved
dégustation	taste, tasting
déjeuner	to lunch; luncheon
déjeuner, petit	breakfast
délice	delight, speciality

55

demi	half
demi-deuil	masked with a white sauce
demi-deuil, salade	with potatoes, truffles and mayonnaise; with cream and mustard
demi-sec	medium dry (of wine)
demi-sel	slightly salted cream cheese
demi-tasse	small cup; coffee-cup
demoiselle	small, eel-like fish
demoiselle de Caen (also demoiselle de Cherbourg or demoiselle de Dieppe)	type of giant shrimp/small lobster
dénoyauté	stoned
derval	with artichoke quarters
dés	thimble, thimble-shaped
descar	with artichoke hearts, chicken, potato croquettes
dés, en	diced
desséché	dried, desiccated
deux	two
diabétique	diabetic
diable	devilled: with rich sauce containing shallots, herbs, wine, Worcester and Harvey sauces
diablotin	round of bread with white sauce and cheese browned under the grill
Diane, sauce	with vegetables, herbs and cream
Diane, steak	thinly cut steak, fried
dieppoise	with mussels and shrimps
digestif	aid to digestion, eg. a liqueur, brandy etc.
dijonnaise	with mustard sauce
dijonnaise, sorbet	blackcurrant water-ice with cassis liqueur
dinde	young hen turkey
dindon	turkey cock
dindonneau	young turkey
dîner	to dine; dinner
dîner sur l'herbe	to picnic
diplomate, pouding	layered sponge, custard cream and fruit dessert

diplomate, sauce	fish and oyster sauce garnished with truffles and diced lobster
dix	ten
dizaine	about ten
Docteur Jules Guyot	very juicy variety of pear
Docteur Morère	variety of strawberry
dodine	boned and stuffed item
dodine de pigeonneau	boned, stuffed and roasted pigeon
dolmades or dolmas	stuffed vine or cabbage leaves
donax	a tiny fish, a fleon
donzelle	small, flat, eel-like fish
dorade	sea-water fish with golden glints in its scales; sea-bream
dorade rouge	red sea bream
doré/ée	golden, gilded
dorée	John Dory, St. Pierre, delicate fleshed fish
Doria	with celeriac, truffles, asparagus tips, beetroot and hard-boiled egg
double	European chub
double-crème	a rich cream cheese
douce, eau	fresh water
doucette	lambs' lettuce, corn salad
douillon	dumpling (fruit)
douillons normande	apples or pears baked in pastry; turnovers
doux/douce	sweet
douzaine	dozen
douze	twelve
doyenné	very sweet variety of pear
doyenné blanc	a long-keeping variety of pear
doyenné de Comice	Comice pear
doyenné de juillet	variety of pear
doyenné d'hiver	a musky-flavoured pear
dragée	sugared almond
draine	missel-thrush, edible bird
droz, jambon	smoked ham from Jura
Dubarry	with cauliflower
dubley	with duchesse potatoes and mushrooms

Dubonnet	wine-based apéritif
duchesse d'Angoulême	very sweet variety of pear
duchesse, pommes	purée of potatoes with added egg yolk
duclair, canard	type of duck
Dugléré	with wine, tomatoes, onions, parsley and cream
dur	hard
duroc	with small new potatoes browned in butter
dur, oeuf	hard-boiled egg
duse	with french beans, tomatoes and parmentier potatoes
duxelles	a kind of mushroom hash
duxelles	with mushrooms, onions and shallots
duxelles, sauce	with onions, white wine, mushrooms and tomatoes
eau	water
eau de fleur d'oranger	orange-flower water
eau-de-vie	brandy
eau douce	fresh, soft water
eau fraîche	cold water
eau minérale	bottled mineral water
eau rougie	water with a dash of red wine
écarlaté	pickled, salted (of pork or beef)
échalote	shallot, scallion
échaudé	pastry made with water-poached dough
échine	chine, backbone cut of meat
éclair	long cream-filled choux pastry
éclade	mussels with pine needles
écorce de citron	lemon peel
écorce d'orange	orange peel
écossaise, sauce	cream sauce with vegetables and french beans
écrevisse	freshwater crayfish
Edam	a hard Dutch cheese
églefin or égrefin	haddock
égyptienne, salade	with rice, chicken livers, ham, mushrooms and artichoke hearts

elbot	a white fleshed fish
embeurré de choux	butter-boiled cabbage
embrocher	to cook on a spit
émincer	to slice (meat)
émincés	slices of meat re-heated in gravy
emmenthal	a hard Swiss cheese
encornet	calamar, squid
endive	chicory
enfariné	floured
entrecôte	rib of beef; steak cut from rib of beef
entrecôte minute	thin rib steak
entrecuisse	the fleshy thigh of poultry or game
entrée	the third course on a full menu
entrelardé	(of bacon) streaky
entremets	side dish; dessert
entremets sucrés	dessert
épaule	shoulder
épaule d'agneau	shoulder of lamb
épeautre, soupe d'	spelt (a type of wheat) soup from Provence
éperlans	smelts, sparling
épi de maïs	sweetcorn
epice	spice
épicéa	a pine-flavoured liqueur from the Jura
épice, pain d'	gingerbread
épicerie	grocer's shop
épigramme	a white lamb stew
épigramme d'agneau	portion of lamb, egg and breadcrumbed and fried
épinards	spinach
épinards au naturel	plain boiled spinach
épinards en branches	leaf spinach
épine d'hiver	a variety of winter pear
épinée	dialect name for chine of pork
épinoche	stickleback, small insipid river fish
épipiner	to de-seed, remove the pips from
épluché	peeled
époisses	a whole-milk, soft cheese from Burgundy
équile	sand eel; small fish cooked as smelt

érable, sucre d'	maple sugar
ercé	a cheese made in the Ariège district
ervy	a soft cheese made in the Champagne area
érythrin	generic name for several varieties of fish
Esaü, purée	with lentils
escabèche d'hareng	cooked, marinated herring
escalope	flattened slice of meat or fish
escargot	snail
escargot de mer	a winkle
Escoffier, sauce	commercially made sauce for flavouring
espadon	swordfish
espagnole	with onions and tomatoes
espagnole, sauce	a basic brown sauce
esquinado	a Provençal name for the spider-crab; crabs cooked with mussels, served in crab shells
estouffade	a stew, a slow-cooked braised dish
estouffat	a stew of pork and beans (Languedoc)
estragon	tarragon
esturgeon	sturgeon
étouffade	a stew, a slow-cooked braised dish
étouffée, à l'	braised
étourdeau	a young capon
étourneau	starling
étrier	stirrup-cup; hot drink
étrille	swimming-crab
étuvé	stewed; a semi-hard Dutch cheese
étuvée, à l'	stewed, braised or steamed (of potatoes etc.)
éventail	fan-shaped
Eve, salade	with apples, bananas, pineapple and cream
Evian	a still spa water
Excelsior	with braised lettuce and fondant potatoes; a cheese from Normandy
exocet	a flying fish
Express	espresso coffee
extrait	extract

faim	hunger
faîne	beechnut
faisan	pheasant
faisandé	high, gamey (of meat)
faisane	hen pheasant
faisselle	a fresh cream cheese served with fruit(s)
faitout	stewpan
fanchette, salade	with chicken, mushrooms, chicory and truffles
fanes de navets	turnip-tops
fanfre	pilot fish
far, far breton	a light batter flan containing raisins or prunes
farce	stuffing; forcemeat
farci	stuffed; a savoury vegetable loaf, speciality of Poitou; a light batter flan/far
farcidures	buckwheat flour and beetroot balls, cooked wrapped in cabbage leaves
farçon	sweet pudding made from potatoes
farée	stuffed cabbage
farine	flour, meal
farine de maïs	cornflour
farineux	floury
faro	a Brussels beer
far poitevin	a herb and vegetable stuffing wrapped in cabbage or lettuce leaves
farz	dumpling
faséole	a type of haricot bean

faubonne	a thick soup of white beans and vegetables
fausse tortue, potage de	mock turtle soup made from calves' heads
faux-filet	sirloin, porterhouse steak
favart	with chicken quenelles, tarragon and mushrooms
faverolle or faverotte	haricot bean
faviole	haricot bean
favorite	with foie gras, asparagus and truffles; with artichoke hearts, celery and roast potatoes
favorite, purée	purée of french beans
favorite, salade	with asparagus tips, crayfish and white truffles
fayot	haricot/kidney bean
fécule	starch
fécule de maïs	cornflour; cornstarch
fédora	with asparagus tartlets, turnips, chestnuts
felignie	variety of early autumn peach
fenouil	fennel, an aniseed-flavoured vegetable
fenouillet	an aniseed-flavoured variety of apple
fenouillette	an aniseed flavoured liqueur
fenugrec	fenugreek, an asiatic herb used in curries
féouse	an egg, bacon and cream tart, a quiche
féra	a salmon-like fish
ferchuse	a stew of pluck, a Burgundian dish
fermière	with root vegetables; a pot roast
ferval	with artichoke hearts, ham, potato croquettes
festin	feast, banquet
feu	fire, oven
feu d'enfer, fruits	mixed poached fruits, flamed with brandy
feu follet, fruits	mixed poached fruits, flamed with brandy
feuillantines	puff pastries
feuille de Dreux	a cheese from the Île de France

feuilles	leaves
feuilleté	in flaky pastry
feuilleton	braised layered veal or pork with stuffing
fève	bean
fève de cacao	cocoa-nib
fève de Lima	lima bean
fève des marais	broad bean
fève jaune	wax bean
fève, petite	wax bean
fève verte	string bean
févrole	small type of broad bean
fiatole	a Mediterranean fish similar to the turbot
ficelle	long, very thin French loaf; very thin pancake
fiélas	name given to the conger eel in Provence
Figaro	with breadcrumbed creamed potatoes and carrots
figatelli	a Corsican pigs'-liver sausage
figue	fig
figuier de barbarie	prickly pear
fijadone	a Corsican flan
filet	fillet, undercut of beef sirloin
filet de citron	a dash of lemon
filet de volaille	slice of breast of poultry
filet, faux-	sirloin, porterhouse steak
filet mignon	small cut from the end of the beef fillet
filtre, café	filtered coffee
financière	with cocks' kidneys, cockscombs, mushrooms, truffles
financière, sauce	rich brown sauce made with madeira wine and truffles
fin de siècle	a cheese made in Normandy
fines de claires	a type of small oyster
fines herbes	a mixture of garden herbs
finte	a fish similar to shad
fissurelle	a limpet-like mollusc
fistulane	a headless mollusc

fladene	a vanilla flavoured cheese tart, speciality of Corsica
flageolet	flageolet or kidney-bean
flamande	with cabbage, carrot and diced pork; a hot-pot
flamande, salade	with chicory, potato, onions, salt herrings
flambé	flamed in brandy or other spirit
flamiche	a leek tart made in Burgundy or Picardy; a flan
flamique	a leek tart from Northern France
flamri	a cold semolina pudding served with red fruits
flamusse	a flan with a cheese-flavoured cream filling
flamuse aux pommes	special apple flan from Nivernais
flan	an open tart; baked custard
flanchet	flank of beef
flangnarde	a lemon or vanilla flavoured flan from Limousin
flendre	flounder
fleuriste	with stuffed tomatoes and roast potatoes
flet	flounder
flétan	halibut
fleur	flower
fleur de Decauville	a cheese from the Île de France
fleur de muscade	mace
fleuron	small flaky pastry garnish
flie	edible limpet/barnacle
flognarde	a lemon or vanilla flavoured flan from Limousin
flondre	flounder
Florence, consommé	thin soup garnished with truffles and vermicelli
Florentin, Saint	a fresh cream cheese from Burgundy
florentine	with spinach
Florida, salade	with fresh fruit and celery
Florian	with braised lettuce, carrots, onions and potatoes

flottantes, îles	light dessert of poached egg whites in custard
floute	croquette made with creamed potatoes
flûte	long, thin loaf
foie	liver
foie de canard	ducks' liver
foie gras, pâté de	truffled goose liver
foie de morue, huile de	cod liver oil
fonds de veau	a veal meat glaze/jelly
fonds d'artichauts	artichoke hearts
fonds de café	coffee grounds
fondue	a dish of melted cheese and herbs
fondue de Franche Comté	a cheese fondue made with eggs
fontaine	spring, well
fontainebleau	a succulent cream cheese; with duchesse potatoes and vegetables
fontine	a cheese
forestière	with morels, bacon and diced, fried potatoes
fort	strong
fouace	flat cake baked on the hearth
fouée	a cream flan filled with bacon; a flat girdle cake
fouetté	whipped, beaten (of eggs or cream)
fougères	a type of Brie, a soft cream cheese
four, au	cooked in the oven; roast, baked
fourme d'Ambert	a fruity-flavoured blue cheese from Auvergne
fourme de Laguiole	a very strong cows'-milk cheese
fourme de Salers	a hard, strong Auvergne cheese
fourré	stuffed, filled with
fourré, chocolat à crème	a chocolate cream sweet
fraîche or frais	fresh
fraise	strawberry
fraises des bois	wild strawberries
fraise de veau	calves' intestines
framboise	raspberry
framboisé	raspberry-flavoured
framboise, ronce	loganberry

française	with spinach and anna potatoes; with mixed vegetables including lettuce and asparagus
france	large, flavoursome peach
francillon, salade	with mussels, potatoes and truffles
frangipane	almond flavoured patisserie; jasmine flavour
frappé	chilled, on ice
frascati or fraucati	with foie gras, asparagus and truffles
fredo, semi	a fruit charlotte
freneuse	with turnips
fréssure	pluck (lights, heart, entrails) of lamb, pig, etc.
freux	crows, rooks
friandises	delicacies, titbits
friands aux écrevisses	crayfish puffs
fricadelle	meat and potato rissole; meat ball
fricandeau	rump (topside) of veal; braised loin of veal
fricassé	poultry cooked in a rich white sauce
fricot	made-up dish, stew
fricoté	stewed
frigadelle	meat and potato rissole
frinot	cheese from the Orléans district
frisé/ée	curly
frisée, chicorée	endive
frisée, laitue	curly lettuce
frit	fried
fritelle	a Corsican cheese fritter
frites	chips, french fried potatoes
fritons	rough pâté, terrine
fritots	meat or poultry fritters
friture	mixture of small fried fish
froid	cold
fromage	cheese
fromage à la crème	cream cheese
fromage à la pie	fresh, unfermented cheese
fromage battu	fresh cream cheese
fromage blanc	a fresh cream cheese
fromage de chèvre	goats'-milk cheese

fromage de cochon	brawn
fromage de tête	pig's cheese, brawn
fromage d'Italie	a dish made from pigs' livers
fromage d'oeufs	cold, soft-baked eggs masked with mayonnaise flavoured with chives, parsley and tarragon
fromage fondu	processed cheese
fromage fort	strong cheese
fromage industriel	processed cheese
fromage persillé	blue-veined cheese
fromagère	a cheese from Franche Comté
fromagerie	shop selling mainly cheeses
froment	wheat
fromenteau	a variety of dessert grape
froment, pain de	first quality wheaten bread
fruit	fruit
fruits candis	candied fruits
fruits, compôte de	stewed, poached fruits
fruits confits	preserved fruits
fruits, corbeille de	basket, selection of fruits
fruits de mer	seafood
fruits, rafraîchis	fruit salad, poached fruits
fruits, salade de	fresh fruit salad
fumé	smoked, cured

gade or gadelle	redcurrant
gaillet	cheese rennet
galantine	boned poultry or meat, stuffed, pressed and jellied
galette	girdle cake; cake made from flaky pastry
galette de pommes de terre	potato cake
galette Pérougienne	a round, flat, solid cake served with cream
galichous	little iced almond cakes
galicien	pistachio-flavoured dessert or cake
gallimaufry	a chicken stew
galopins	bread pancakes from Picardy
gamba	a large prawn
gambra	a type of partridge
ganga	hazel-grouse
gantois	Flemish pastries
gaperon	a cheese
garbure	a thick vegetable soup/stew
gardon	a small roach
gardon rouge	a freshwater, roach-like fish
garenne, lapin de	wild rabbit
garni	garnish, garnished with
gastrochère	type of mollusc
gastronome	with truffles, chestnuts, morels, asparagus
gâteau	cake, open tart
gâteau aux pommes	apple tart, apple cake

68

gâteau basque	tart with almond paste and jam
gâteau Beauvilliers	sponge-cake with kirsch and cream
gâteau de riz	stiff rice pudding
gâteau des Rois	Twelfth Night cake
gâteau de miel	honeycomb
gâteaux de Noël	mincepies
gaude	maize-flour porridge or pudding
gaufre	waffle
gaufre fourrée	waffle with filling
gaufrette	wafer biscuit
gauloise	with truffles, mushrooms, crayfish; with chickens' kidneys, truffles, cockscombs
gayette	flat sausage of pork liver and bacon
gazeuse	aerated, fizzy
gazpacho	a cold, high-flavoured tomato soup
geai	jay, an edible bird
gebie	a small shellfish
gelée	jelly
gelées d'entremets	sweet jellies
gelée de pommes	apple jelly
gelée de viande	meat jelly, savoury jelly
gelée, en	in jelly, jellied
gêline de Touraine	a small blackish edible fowl
gelinotte	hazel grouse, hazel hen
gendarme	pickled herring; dry hard Swiss sausage
Genéral Chanzy	variety of strawberry
genevoise	flavoured with red wine
genevrette	juniper wine
genièvre	juniper
génisse	ox, young heifer
génoise	Genoese sponge
georgette	stuffed with crayfish tails
germigny	a Burgundian cheese
germon	tunny fish, tuna
Géromé	a very strong cheese made from cows' milk
gervais	a creamy, unsalted cheese
gésier	gizzard
gex	a blue-veined cheese from Jura

gibassier	traditional Provençal cake
gibelotte	stew of hare or rabbit
gibier	game
gibier à plume	feathered game
gibier à poil	furred game
gibier d'eau	wildfowl
gigorit	lamb's pluck
gigot, gigotin	leg (of mutton)
gigue	haunch of venison or game
gimblette	ring-biscuit, cookie
gingembre	ginger
gingembre confit	candied ginger
girasol	sunflower
girelle	a delicately-flavoured seafish similar to eel
girofle	clove
girol or girolle	chanterelle, mushroom
gîte	leg of beef
gîte à la noix	silverside of beef
givré	frosted (usually used of a cake)
glace	ice-cream; glaze
glaçon	ice cube
glaire	egg white
glanis	wels, a freshwater fish
Gloria	coffee served with spirits
Gloucester, sauce	mayonnaise with sour cream and Escoffier sauce
glux	a cheese from the Nivernais area
gniole	rum, brandy
gnocchi, or gnokis	gnocchi
gobie	a small fish
godard	with quenelles, sweetbreads, truffles and chickens' kidneys
godard, sauce	with champagne, vegetables and mushroom essence
godiveau	veal and fat forcemeat
goéland	a large seagull
gogue	bacon rolls stuffed with vegetables
goguette	highly spiced flat sausage
gombaut or gombo	okra, ladies' fingers

gorenflot	with red cabbage and savoy sausage (a spicy sausage from Panay)
goret	piglet over six months old
gorge	throat, neck
gorge de pigeon	pigeon's breast
gorgonzola	a strong blue cheese
gouda	a whole-milk Dutch cheese
gouère aux pommes	apples cooked in batter
gouffé	with asparagus, morels and duchesse potatoes
gougère	cheese-enriched choux pastry
gougnette	type of hot doughnut
goujon	small gudgeon fish
goujonnettes	small fried fillets of fish
goujonnière or perche goujonnière	small gudgeon, ruff
goulasch	Hungarian style stew
goura	squab, crown-pigeon
gourde	gourd
gourilos	endive stalks
gourmandises	dainties, sweetmeats
gournay	a soft, whole-milk Normandy cheese
gousse	pod, shell, husk
gousse d'ail	clove of garlic
goût	taste, flavour
goutte	drop (of liquid or flavouring)
goutte d'or, prune	golden egg plum
goyave	guava
goyère	tart, flan
grain	grain, seed
grain d'anis	aniseed
grain de café	coffee bean
grain de carvi	caraway seed
grain de pavot	poppyseed
grain de poivre	peppercorn
grain de raisin	grape
grain, poulet de	corn-fed pullet; spring chicken
graisse	fat, dripping
graisse de porc	lard
graisse de rognons	suet

graisse de rôti	dripping
Grand Duc	with asparagus, truffles and crayfish tails
Grand Veneur	sauce for game with redcurrant jelly, wine and cream
granité	grainy water-ice
grapiaux	large pancakes cooked in pork fat
gras(se)	fat meat; rich food
gras-double	tripe
gras, potage	meat soup
gratin, au	cooked with breadcrumbs and cheese
gratin dauphinois	sliced potatoes cooked with cream and garlic
gratiné	breadcrumbed; cooked with cheese
gratinée	onion soup with cheese
gravenche	fish of the salmon family
gréaves	crackling
grecque, à la	cooked and steeped in wine, spices and herbs
grecque, à la, sauce	fish velouté with onion, celery, fennel and cream
gremille	species of perch, gudgeon, ruff or pope
grenade	pomegranate
grenadier	a white-fleshed fish
grenadin	small slice of fillet of veal
grenadine	grenadine, or grenadine syrup
grenouille	frog
grenouilles, cuisses de	frogs' legs
gribiche, sauce	mayonnaise with mustard, capers, gherkins
gril	grid-iron, grill
grillade	grilled meat, especially steak
grillade de pain	toast
grillage	grilling, boiling, toasting
grillée, tarte	latticed tart or flan
Grimaldi, consommé	thin chicken soup with tomatoes and celeriac
griotte	morello cherry
gris, petits	tiny snails
grive	thrush

grog	hot drink with lemon and rum or brandy
grondin	gurnard, fish similar to red mullet
gros(se)	large, big
gros-blanquet	variety of pear
groseille	currant, gooseberry
groseille à grappe	redcurrant, whitecurrant
groseille à maquereau	gooseberry
groseille noire	blackcurrant
groseille rouge	redcurrant
gros sel	coarse salt
grosse-mignonne	large sweet variety of peach
grotte-paille	a variety of Brie cheese
grous or groux	buckwheat gruel
grouse	grouse
gruau	finest wheat flour, gruel
gruau d'avoine	groats, oatmeal
gruau, pain de	finest wheaten bread
grumeau	finely separated curds
gruyère	a hard cheese
gryphée	Portuguese oyster
guerbigny	a cheese made in Guéret
guigne	a red or white cherry
guignette	a name given to the winkle in Aunis; sandpiper
guignolet	cherry brandy
guillaret	a hard biscuit
guimauve	marshmallow
gymnètre	fish similar to cod

haché	finely chopped
haché menu	minced
haché, steack	beefburger
hachis	mince, hash
haddock	smoked haddock
halicot de mouton	mutton stew with beans
haliotide or haliotis	ormer, a shell-fish
hampe	flank of beef; breast of venison; rolled, spiced pork breast
hanche	haunch
hareng	herring
hareng bouffi	bloater
hareng fumé	kipper
hareng pec	freshly salted, unsmoked herring
hareng salé	bloater
harenguet	sprat; sardine
haricots beurre	white french beans
haricots blancs	haricot beans
haricots de Lima	green lima beans
haricot de mouton	Irish stew; mutton stew with beans
haricots d'Espagne	scarlet runner beans
haricots flageolets	flageolet beans
haricots rouges	red haricot/kidney beans
haricots verts	french beans
helianthé	sunflower
Hélène, fruits	fruits served with ice-cream and hot chocolate sauce
Hélène, poire Belle	pear with chocolate sauce and ice-cream
helvelle	edible mushroom, similar to morel

hénons	local name for cockles (Picardy)
herbe	herb
herbes, fines	assorted herbs
herbes potagères	pot-herbs
héricart	variety of strawberry
Hermine, salade	with chicken, celery and chicory
hiver	winter
hiver, salade d'	winter salad
hochepot	hotpot
hochequeue	small edible bird, wagtail
hollandaise, sauce	an egg yolk and butter sauce
Hollande, fromage de	Dutch cheese
homard	lobster
homard épineux	crayfish
hongrois	Hungarian
hongroise	spicy flavour, usually with paprika
hornet	variety of raspberry
houblon, jets de	hop shoots, hop sprouts
huile	oil
huile blanche	poppyseed oil
huile d'amandes	almond oil
huile d'arachide	peanut oil
huile de copra(h)	coconut oil
huile de foie de morue	cod liver oil
huile de girofle	oil of cloves
huile de maïs	corn oil
huile de navette	rapeseed oil
huile de palme	palm oil
huile d'oeillette	poppyseed oil
huit	eight
huître	oyster
huître plat	flat oyster
huître portugaise	chunky oyster
huître en coquilles	scalloped oysters
huîtrier	oyster-catcher, edible bird similar to plover
huppe	tufted lark, an edible bird
huppemeau	a cheese similar to brie
hure	boar's head; brawn; potted boar's head
hure de brochet	galantine of jellied pike

hure de sanglier	boar's head
hussarde	with horseradish, aubergines and potatoes
hydromel	mead, a drink made from honey
icaque	coco-plum, a fruit
igname	yam
îles flottantes	dessert of poached egg whites in custard
impératrice	usually with rice
impériale	variety of plum; with truffles, foie gras and kidneys
impéria, salade	with asparagus tips, truffles and lettuce
incheville	a cheese from Normandy
indienne	curry flavoured
iridée	a variety of edible seaweed
Isabelle, salade	with truffles, celery, mushrooms, artichoke hearts and potatoes
Ismail Bayeedi	with aubergines, rice and tomatoes
issues	pluck, i.e. lights, hearts, entrails, etc.
italienne	with assorted vegetables and spaghetti or macaroni
ivoire	with cream sauce and mushrooms
Izarra	a herb and flower liqueur

Jacques	pancakes with an apple filling
Jacques, coupe	fruit salad with ice-cream
jalousies	little flaky-pastry cakes
jamble	an edible limpet/barnacle
jambon	ham
jambon de Bayonne	a mild ham marinated in wine
jambon blanc	boiled ham
jambon crû	raw ham
jambon de Toulouse	salted and diced ham eaten raw
jambon droz	smoked ham from the Jura region
jambonette	a type of sausage or terrine
jambon fumé	smoked ham
jambon glacé	glazed ham served cold
jambonneau	knuckle of ham; hand of pork
jambon persillé	ham set in a parsley jelly
japonaise	with Japanese artichokes; an iced bombe dessert; a patisserie made with almonds and egg whites; a deep oyster
japonaise, salade	with potatoes, mussels and celery
jardin, du	from the garden
jardinière	mixed diced vegetables
jarret	knuckle of veal; shin of beef
jaseur	waxwing, an edible bird
jaune d'oeuf	yolk of egg
javanaise, salade	with oranges, sour cream and horseradish
Jean-Doré	John Dory, a fish
jesse	small, bony river fish
jessica	with artichokes, bone marrow, mushrooms, shallots

jésuite	a small flaky pastry
jésus	a type of pork-liver sausage
jets de houblon	hop sprouts, hop shoots
jocasse	missel thrush
joinville	with mushrooms, shrimps and truffles
jonchée	cream cheese from Aunis
jubliée, cerises	poached cherries flamed in brandy
judic	with tomatoes, lettuce and château potatoes
Jules Duyot	a juicy variety of pear
Jules Verne	with potatoes, turnips and mushrooms
julienne	finely shredded vegetable garnish; ling fish
jus	juice; gravy; roasting liquor
jus d'orange	orange juice
jussière	with onions, lettuces and carrots
kaki	persimmon, a fruit
kalerii	type of pork brawn (Alsace)
kaltschale	a rich fruit salad with liqueurs
keftede	veal or pork and potato rissole
keftes-kebab	kebab
kig ha farz	beef stew with dumplings (Brittany)
kilkis	Norwegian anchovies
kina lilet	a wine-based apéritif
kir	a blackcurrant and wine cocktail
kirke	a dark violet variety of plum
kirsch	a cherry-flavoured liqueur
kneplfe	a fritter (Alsace)
koulibiak	a hot fish pie
kromeskies	little meat balls
kummel	cumin-flavoured liqueur
kumquat	a variety of tiny orange

labre	labrus, wrasse, sea-fish used in soups and stews
lache	a small delicate sea-fish
lagopède	grouse
lagopède, rouge	red grouse
laguipière, sauce	a fish-flavoured egg and lemon sauce
lait	milk
laitances	soft roes
lait battu	buttermilk
lait, cochon de	sucking-pig
lait condensé	condensed milk
lait d'ânesse	asses' milk
lait de beurre	buttermilk
lait de poule	egg-nog
lait desséché	dried milk
lait fermenté	fermented milk
laitiat	drink of fruits mixed with whey
lait, petit	whey
laitue	lettuce
laitue pommée	cabbage lettuce
laitue romaine	cos lettuce
lakmé, salade	curry-flavoured with tomatoes, peppers, rice
Lamballe	with mushrooms, truffles, port and cream
lamelles	flakes
lamproie	lamprey, eel-like fish
lampsane	nipplewort, lampsana
lançon	sand-eel, small fish cooked like a smelt
langouste	sea crayfish, spiny lobster
langoustine	Dublin Bay prawn; scampi
langue	tongue

79

langue-de-chat	thin, flat finger biscuit
languedocienne	with mushrooms, aubergines and fried potatoes
lanière	strip
lapereau	young wild rabbit
lapin	rabbit
lapin de clapier	domestic rabbit
lapin de garenne	wild rabbit
lard	bacon
lardons	pieces of bacon
lasagnes	lasagne, Italian pasta dish
laumes, les	a cheese from Burgundy
laurier	bay, a herb
Lavallière	with truffles, lambs' sweetbreads and crayfish
lavaret	a salmon-like lake fish
lavasse	thin, watery soup or wine
lèche	thin slice of meat or bread
légume	vegetable
légumes secs	dried vegetables
légumes verts	green vegetables
lentilles	lentils, mung beans
lépidostée	gar-pike, a freshwater fish
lépiote	an edible fungus
letchi	lychee, a Chinese fruit
levain, pain sans	unleavened bread
levraut	leveret, young hare
levroux	a goat cheese
levure	yeast
liard	coin-shaped
libre-service	self-service
liche	a tuna-like fish
liégeoise	flavoured with juniper
lieu	a type of whiting, pollack
lièvre	hare
lièvre, civet de	jugged hare
lièvre, râble de	saddle of hare
ligurienne	with tomatoes, rizotto and duchesse potatoes
limande	dab, lemon sole

limandelle	a flat, plaice-like fish
lime, jus de	lime juice
limette	sweet lime
limon	sour lime
limonade	fizzy lemonade
limousine	with red cabbage
lingue	ling, fish of the cod family
linot(te)	linnet, small edible bird
liqueur	liquor, drink
liqueur de dessert	liqueur
liqueur douce	soft drink
lisette	a small fish
lit	bed, base
litre	litre, about one and three-quarters of a pint
livarot	a strong soft cheese from Normandy
livèche	lovage, a herb
livonienne	a fish sauce with carrots, truffles and parsley
loche	loach, a freshwater fish
loir	edible dormouse
longchamp	broth with sorrel, vermicelli and peas
longe	top part of loin of veal or venison
longuet	bread stick
lonzo	raw salted, herb-flavoured pork
lorette	with chicken croquettes, asparagus, truffles
lorette, salade	corn salad with celery and beetroot
loriot	golden oriole, small edible bird
lorraine	with red cabbage braised in red wine
losange	lozenge, lozenge-shaped
lotte or lotte de rivière	burbot, barbot, eel-pout
lotte de mer	monk-fish, angel fish
loubine	regional name for grey mullet
louise-bonne	variety of late pear
louisette, salade	with cos lettuce, tomatoes and grapes
loup or loup de mer	sea-bass, sea-perch, sea-dace
lou trebuc	preserved goose or pork
luzerne	alfalfa
lyonnaise	with onions

macaron	macaroon, almond cake
macaronade	beef stew with noodles
macconet	a small goat cheese
macédoine	fruit or vegetables cut into dice
macédoine de fruits	fruit salad
macédoine de légumes	vegetable salad
macéré	soaked, steeped
mâche	corn salad, lambs' lettuce
macis	mace, dried shell of nutmeg
mâconnaise	flavoured with red wine
macreuse	strong-flavoured wild duck; lean meat found on shoulder of beef
madeleine	small sponge-cake
madère	madeira wine
madère, gâteau au	tipsy-cake
madrilène	with tomatoes; tomato-flavoured
magistère	a type of soup
magret	fillet, slice of breast
maharadjah, salade	curry-flavoured with crab, celeriac, courgettes
maigre	thin, lean
maillot	with carrots, turnips, beans and lettuce
Maintenon	with a creamy white mushroom or truffle sauce
maïs	maize, corn
maïs, farine de	maize-flour, cornflour
maître d'hôtel	butter with salt, pepper, lemon juice and parsley
Malakoff	a cheese

Malakoff, pouding	a vanilla custard cream with mincemeat
malard	mallard, wild duck
maltaise, sauce	egg and butter sauce with juice of blood oranges
mamirolle	an oblong-shaped cheese from Jura
manchon	small cream-filled pastry
mandarine	tangerine
mange-tout	sugar pea with edible pod
manicamp	a cheese from Picardy
mangue	mango, an East Indian fruit
manon, salade	with lettuce, grapefruit and lemon juice
manqué	a type of sponge cake
mante de mer	squill-fish, a crustacean
maquereau	mackerel
maraîchère	with salsify, carrots, onions, potatoes, artichokes
marasquin	maraschino, a cherry liqueur
marbré	marbled, marble design
marc	a rough brandy
marcassin	young wild boar
Marcellin, St	flat, creamy cheese from the French Alps
marchand de vin	with red wine sauce
marché	market
maréchal	with asparagus tips and truffles
marengo	with crayfish, eggs and brandy
marenne	variety of oyster
mariage	thick meat soup with fish garnish (Provence)
mariette, fruits	poached fruits flavoured with rum
marignan	sponge cake with apricot jam and meringue
marigny	with artichoke hearts, sweetcorn and potatoes
marinade	liquid for pickling, sousing or steeping
mariné	marinated
marinière	with onion, wine and parsley sauce
marivaux	with duchesse potatoes and mixed vegetables

marjolaine	sweet marjoram, a herb
marmelade	compote of fruits; stewed fruits
marmelade d'oignons	a spicy onion pickle
marmelade d'oranges	orange marmalade
marmite	stew, stock-pot
marmite dieppoise	fish stew; thick fish soup
marmite, petite	meat and vegetable soup
marocaine	with rice, courgettes, sweet peppers
maroille(s) or marolle(s)	a brownish, rich-flavoured cheese
marouette	rail, a small bird
marquise	very sweet variety of pear
marquise au chocolat	rich chocolate sponge cake with cream
marrons	sweet chestnuts
marrons glacés	candied chestnuts
martin-sec	a gritty variety of pear
martin-sire	a variety of pear
marvel	type of dessert fritter
mascotte	with artichoke hearts, truffles and potatoes; Genoese cake filled with hazelnut cream
masqué	masked with, covered with
masséna	with artichoke hearts and bone marrow
massenet	with artichokes, french beans, anna potatoes
massepain	marzipan; marzipan-flavoured cake/ biscuit
massillons	a small petit-four in tartlet shape
matefaim	a thick, nourishing pancake
matelote or matelotte	a fish stew; with onions and mush-rooms
matignon	artichoke hearts and lettuce garnish
maubèche	sandpiper
mauviette	lark
mayonnaise	cold dish with mayonnaise and salad
mayonnaise, sauce	rich cold sauce made from egg yolks, oil and vinegar
mazagran	black coffee in a glass; tartlet lined with potatoes with various fillings; various fillings sandwiched between layers of creamed potatoes

mazarin	Genoese sponge with crystallized fruit filling
médaillon	meat cut into medallion shape
mélange	mixture
mélasses	molasses, treacle
mélasse raffinée	golden syrup
melba	fruit served with ice-cream and raspberry sauce; garnished with stuffed tomatoes and braised lettuce
melba, toast	very thin, crisp toast
mélilot	a fragrant herb
méli-mélo	hotch-potch, mixture of items
mélisse	lemon balm, lemon mint
melon	melon
melon confit	crystallized melon
melon d'eau	watermelon
melon de Malabar	Siamese pumpkin
mélongène	aubergine, eggplant
mendiant	spiced cherry cake
mendiants, quatre	dessert of almonds, figs, hazelnuts, raisins
menthe	mint
menthe anglaise	peppermint
menthe, crème de	peppermint liqueur
menthe crépue	curly mint
menthe poivrée	peppermint
menthe rouge	red mint
menthe verte	spearmint, garden mint
mentonnaise	with courgettes, artichokes, rice, olives
menu	very small
mer	sea
mère de sole	fish similar to plaice
mer, fruits de	seafood
merguez	a highly-spiced sausage
meringue glacée	meringue with ice cream
meringue Chantilly	meringue with Chantilly cream
merise	gean, wild cherry
merlan	whiting, hake
merle	blackbird
merlu	hake, colin

merluche	dried hake; dried, unsalted cod
mérou	a rather tasteless sea fish
merveille	marvel: a pastry fritter
merveille de quatre saisons	a variety of raspberry
mesclun	a mixture of salad leaves
messire-jean	very fragrant variety of pear
metton	cheese from the Jura mountains
meuils	name for grey mullet (Aunis)
meunier	chub, freshwater fish
meunière	cooked in butter with lemon juice and parsley
meurette	type of thick fish or veal stew
miche	round cob loaf
Michelaine	liqueur made at Mont St. Michel
micisca	dish of marinated smoked pork (Corsica)
midinette, salade	with apples, chicken, celery, gruyère cheese
miel	honey
miellé	honeyed, sweetened or flavoured with honey
migliassis	variety of Corsican cake
mignonette	coarsely ground fresh pepper
Mikado	with curried rice; with soya shoots in cream
Mikado, salade	with shrimps, chrysanthemum petals, tomatoes and sweet peppers
milanaise	small, aniseed-flavoured cakes; fried in breadcrumbs; with macaroni or spaghetti
miliase	a kind of porridge, gruel
millard	a type of cherry cake
millas	a thick porridge
millefeuille	layered flaky pastry filled with sweet or savoury filling
milliassous	small pastries made from millet and lemons
millière	maize-meal and rice porridge
mimosa	with hard-boiled egg-yolks

mince	thin
mingaux, Rennes	a kind of cream cheese from Brittany
minute, entrecôte	thin steak
miques de maïs	a type of bread
mirabeau	with olives, anchovies and tarragon
mirabelle	a small, yellow plum
mirepoi	assorted diced vegetables
mirepoi, sauce	with diced celery, onions, carrots and herbs
mirlitons de Rouen	small orange-flower-water flavoured tartlets
miroir, oeufs au	eggs cooked in butter
mironton or miroton	hash
mode, à la	as cooked by, in the style of
moderne	with mixed vegetables
moelle	marrow, bone-marrow
moelle de chicorée	endive stalks, stumps
moelle, os à	marrow-bone
mogettes	red beans (Aunis)
mogettes	french beans with butter and cream (Poitou)
moitié	half
moka	mocha, mocha-coffee flavour
mokatine	small, coffee-flavoured cake
mollet, oeuf	soft-boiled egg
Monaco, consommé	clear chicken broth with cake mixture garnish
mondé	blanched (almonds); stoned (cherries)
monie borgne	variety of cod
Mont Blanc	a cream and chestnut dessert
Mont Bry	with spinach and mushrooms
Mont-Canis	a semi-hard, blue-veined cheese
Mont-de-cats	a cheese from French Flanders
mont d'or	a cheese made from cows' milk from Lyons
montereau	a soft cream cheese, type of brie
montglas	with truffles, foie gras and pickled tongue
montgolfière	in white sauce with truffles and mushrooms

montmorency	variety of cherry; with cherries
montpellier, beurre de	green coloured butter
montpensier	with asparagus tips and truffles
montpensier, gâteau de	flan made with almonds, egg whites and vanilla
monselet	with artichoke hearts and truffles
monsieur, de	variety of plum; a cheese from Normandy
mont ventoux	strong cheese from Provence
moque	a clove flavoured pastry
morbier	a round, cows'-milk cheese from Jura
Morbihan	variety of oyster
morçeau	piece, morsel
morçeaux, sucre en	loaf sugar, sugar lumps
morelle	aubergine, eggplant
morille	morel, type of mushroom
morillon	small, black grape
mornay	with cheese sauce
mornay, sauce	a rich cheese sauce
mortadelle	mortadella, large pork sausage
morue	cod
morue fraîche	fresh cod
morue noire	haddock
morue salée	salt cod
morue St Pierre	haddock
moruette	variety of small fish
Moscovite	dessert similar to Bavarian cream
Moscovite, sauce	vegetable sauce with juniper berries, garnished with almonds and currants
mostelle	delicately-flavoured Mediterranean fish
Mothe	a strong goat cheese
Mothe-Sainte-Héraye	a goat cheese from Poitou
motte de beurre	dish of butter
mou	lights, lungs of certain animals
mouchelet	a cheese made in Picardy
mouclade	mussels cooked in white wine and cream sauce
mouette	gull, bird
mouette, oeufs de	gulls' eggs

mouflon	wild sheep
moules	mussels
moulin	mill
mouloucoutani	mulligatawny soup or dish; curry flavoured
mousquetaire	mayonnaise with shallots, wine, chives, cayenne
moussaka	dish of meat with vegetables and aubergines
mousse	sweet or savoury dish made from pounded ingredients set with gelatine
mousseau	type of bread made from wheaten flour
mousseline	tiny mousse
mousseline, gâteau	spongecake
mousseline, pommes	mashed potatoes
mousseline, sauce	a rich egg and butter sauce with added cream
mousseron	small edible mushroom
mousseux	sparkling, fizzy
moutarde	mustard
moutardelle	a variety of horseradish
mouton	sheep, mutton
moyen	middle, moderate
muge	mullet
muge, barbue	red mullet
mulen	soft creamy cheese, a type of brie
mulet or mulle	grey mullet
munster	very strong cheese usually flavoured with caraway and aniseed
mûre	mulberry
mûre de ronce	blackberry
murène	moray eel
mûre sauvage	blackberry
murois	a cheese
muron	blackberry, wild raspberry
musard, purée	creamed flageolet beans
muscade	nutmeg
muscade, fleur de	mace
muscadelle	a musky-flavoured pear
muscat	muscatel, raisin

museau	brawn
musqué	muscovy duck
musette, boeuf en	rolled, boned shoulder of beef
mustèle	Mediterranean fish similar to burbot
myrtille	bilberry
mystère, glace	ice cream with macaroon centre
nage, à la	shellfish cooked in a herb flavoured liquid
nageoires de tortue	turtle flippers
nanette	with artichoke hearts, lettuce, mushrooms, truffles
nantais	a small almond biscuit; a Breton cheese; a duckling from Nantes
Nantua	with crayfish tails or purée
napolitaine	with horseradish, ham and madeira
napolitaine, sauce	a brown sauce with redcurrant jelly
napolitaine, tranche	slice of ice cream of various flavours
nappé	covered with
natives	oysters
natte	plait, braid
nature	plain, plainly-cooked, simple
nature, pommes	plain boiled potatoes
navarin d'agneau	lamb stew with dumplings, onions, turnips
navet	turnip
navet de suède	swede
navets, fanes de	turnip-tops
navette	rape-seed
navette, huile de	rape-seed oil
nectarine	nectarine
nèfle	medlar
nèfle du Japon	loquat, Japanese medlar
négreska	creme caramel with ice-cream and chocolate sauce
nègre en chemise	chocolate ice-cream covered with whipped cream
nègre, tête de	chocolate coated meringue patisserie
négus	wine spiced with sugar, lemons and nutmeg; a kind of soft caramel

neige	snow
neige de Florence	a delicate pasta used as a garnish for soup
neige, oeufs à la	poached egg whites on vanilla custard
nelusko	small iced petits fours
nelusko, salade	with beetroot, asparagus tips, potatoes
nem	roll of filo pastry with sweet or savoury filling
nemours	small flaky pastry tartlets
neuf	nine
neufchâtel	a cheese from Normandy
nichette	with mushrooms, horseradish, chickens' kidneys
niçoise	with artichokes, olives, tomatoes and garlic
niçoise, salade	with potatoes, french beans, anchovies, capers; olives and tomatoes
nid	nest
nid d'abeilles	honeycomb
ninon	with cockscombs and kidneys, asparagus and duchesse potatoes
niolo	a Corsican cheese
nivernaise	with carrots, onions, turnips, braised lettuce
nivernaise sauce	white wine, butter and garlic sauce
Noël	Christmas
Noël, bûche de	Yule log
Noël, gâteau de	Christmas cake
Noilly, sauce	vermouth sauce
noir	black
noir, beurre	burnt butter; black butter
noir, café	black coffee
noisette	hazelnut; small round slice of meat
noisette d'agneau	the 'eye' of a lamb chop
noisette, sauce	egg and brown butter sauce
noisettes, pommes	small nut-shaped potatoes fried in butter
noisettines	small cakes with marzipan and short pastry
noix	nut, walnut

noix d'acajou	cashew nut
noix d'Amérique	Brazil nut
noix d'arec	betel nut, areca nut
noix de Brésil	Brazil nut
noix de coco	coconut
noix de gigot	'Pope's eye' in leg of mutton
noix de veau	cushion of veal; topside of leg of veal
noix pâtissière	round of veal; chump end of loin of veal
nonat	tiny Mediterranean fish
non-gazeuse	still, not aerated (of drink)
nonnes, salade de	with rice, chicken and truffles
nonnette	iced gingerbread
nonpareilles	small capers pickled in vinegar
normand(e)	from or of Normandy
normande	with oysters, mushrooms, shrimps, mussels; with cider and/or calvados and/or apples
normande, sauce	fish velouté with egg yolks and cream
normande, sorbet	apple water-ice with calvados
norvégienne	dessert of ice cream in a hot meringue casing
nougat	confectionery made with almonds and honey
nougatines	small sponge-cakes layered with praline cream
nouilles	noodles
nouillettes	tiny noodles
nouveau, nouvelle	new, fresh
nouzillards	name for chestnuts in the Loire area
noyau	kernel, stone (of fruit)

oblade	fish similar to bream
oedicnème	stone-curlew, bird similar to plover
oeuf	egg
oeuf à la coq	boiled egg
oeuf à la cuillère	boiled egg
oeufs à la Monteynard	soft-boiled eggs on a bed of rice
oeufs à la neige	poached egg whites in vanilla custard
oeufs bénédictine	poached eggs with hollandaise sauce on a bed of salt cod or pastry
oeufs bourguignonne	eggs poached in red wine
oeufs brouillés	scrambled eggs
oeufs durs	hard-boiled eggs
oeufs en cocotte	eggs baked in ramekins with cream
oeufs en meurette	eggs poached in wine sauce
oeufs frais	new-laid eggs
oeufs maritchu	creamy scrambled eggs served with globe artichokes
oeufs mollets	soft-boiled eggs
oeufs mouillettes	soft-boiled eggs with 'soldiers'
oeufs sur le plat	fried eggs
officier	variety of cod
ognonnade or oignonade	finely chopped onions; stew containing a large proportion of onions
oie	goose
oignon	onion
oignon, petit	pickling onion
oilette, huile d'	poppyseed oil
oille	casserole of meat and vegetables
oiseau	bird

oiseaux sans têtes	slices of meat, stuffed and rolled then cooked gently in a rich sauce
oison	gosling, young goose
olive	olive
olive, huile d'	olive oil
olivet	a ewes'-milk cheese from the Loiret
oloron	a cream cheese
omble chevalier	char, fish similar to salmon-trout
ombre commun	grayling, fish cooked similarly to trout
ombre de mer or ombrine	umbra, umbrine, fish similar to bass
omelette	omelette
omelette à la confiture	sweet omelette
omelette aux fines herbes	herb flavoured omelette
omelette brayaude	omelette with diced potatoes, lean bacon, cream and cheese
omelette Mère Poulard	a fluffy omelette (as made at Mont St Michel)
omelette nivernaise	omelette with sorrel, ham and chives
omelette norvégienne	hot meringue dessert with a centre of ice cream
omelette parmentier	potato omelette
onglet	a long rump steak
onze	eleven
opéra	with chicken livers, asparagus tips and potatoes
orange	orange
orangeade	aerated orange drink
orange amère	bitter/Seville orange
orange, écorce d'	orange peel
orangeat	candied orange peel
oranger, eau de fleur d'	orange flower water
orange pressée	fresh orange juice
oranges, confiture d'	orange marmalade
orangine	sponge pastry flavoured with candied orange peel
oreille	ear
oreiller de la belle Aurore	a grandiose game pie
oreillette	type of fritter
orge	barley

orgeat	beverage made from almonds and sugar
orge perlé	pearl barley
orge, sucre d'	barley sugar
orientale	with rice, okra and tomatoes; with tomatoes, garlic and saffron
orientale, salade	with rice, sweet peppers, tomatoes, black olives
orientale, sauce	lobster sauce with curry and onions
origan	wild marjoram
Orléans, consommé	thin chicken soup garnished with chicken quenelles
Orloff	with celery, tomatoes, lettuce
Orly	(usually of fish) battered, fried and served with tomato sauce
ormeau, ormet or ormier	ormer, a shell-fish
oronge	variety of mushroom
orphie	garfish, snipe-eel
orties, potage crème d'	young nettle soup
ortolan	bunting
os	bone
os à moëlle	marrowbone
oseille	sorrel
osselet	knucklebone (of sheep)
osso bucco	veal stew
oublie	cone-shaped wafer biscuit
ouliat	onion soup
oursin	sea urchin
outarde	bustard
oyornade	goose in red wine
pacane	pecan nut
pagre	fish similar to sea bream
pain	bread; mousse in a loaf shape
pain à l'aillade	slice of toasted garlic bread
pain anglais	sandwich loaf; almond cookie
pain aux noix	walnut bread
pain bis	brown bread
pain complet	wholemeal bread
pain de courgettes	courgette mousse
pain de froment	first quality wheaten bread

pain de mie	sandwich loaf
pain d'épice	gingerbread
pain de poissons	fish loaf
pain de seigle	rye bread
pain de sucre	sugar loaf, lump of sugar
pain de viande	meat loaf
pain frais	new bread
pain grillé	toasted bread
pain hallé	toasted bread
pain moulé	tin loaf
pain perdu	stale bread, dipped in beaten egg and fried
pain, petit	bread roll
pain sans levain	unleavened bread
paladru	a cheese from Savoy
palais de boeuf	ox palate
paleron de boeuf	chuck beef
Palestine, purée	purée of potatoes and Jerusalem artichokes
palet	a patty, flat cake (of potato, etc.)
palette de porc	shoulder of pork
palme	palm
palme, huile de	palm oil
palmier	a small patisserie made from puff pastry
palmier, coeurs de	palm hearts
paloise	with potato balls and french beans; with new vegetables, cauliflower and hollandaise sauce
paloise, sauce	sauce made from eggs, butter, onions and mint
paloise, salade	with artichokes, celeriac, asparagus tips
palombe	wood pigeon
palomet	a variety of edible fungus, russula
palourde	clam; a vegetable squash/marrow
pamplemousse	grapefruit
panaché	plumed, plume-shape; shandy-gaff, a drink
panachée, glace	mixed flavour ice cream
panachée, salade	mixed salad

panachés	with flageolet and french beans
panachées de poissons	dish of assorted tiny fish
panade	a soup-like dish made from bread, milk and cheese
panais	parsnip
pan bagnat	a slice of bread, moistened with olive oil, covered with anchovy fillets, tomatoes, capers
pané	breaded
panetière	dish served in a scooped-out bread case
panettone	an Italian cake
panette dolce	a sweet Corsican raisin bread for Easter
panier	basket
panisso	a porridge of chickpeas fried in oil and eaten with sugar
pannequet	a sweet or savoury type of pancake
pantin	a patty filled with fine pork forcemeat
panure	breadcrumbs
papaya	pawpaw fruit
papier	paper
papier de chine	rice paper
papier de riz	rice paper
papillote	oiled or buttered paper enclosing food while it is cooked
paprika	paprika, a Hungarian pepper red in colour
parfait	a light ice cream
parfait-amour	liqueur flavoured with lemon, cinnamon, coriander
parfum	flavour, perfume
Paris-Brest	a cream-filled, almond-topped pastry ring
parisien	a type of gâteau
parisienne	with braised lettuce and tiny nut-shaped potatoes; with artichokes, tongue, truffles
parisienne, salade	vegetable salad with lobster and truffles
parisienne, sauce	pounded cream cheese with salt, paprika, oil and lemon juice
parmentier(ière)	with potatoes

parmentine	a jacket-baked potato
parmesan	a very hard Italian cheese
parmesane	with parmesan cheese
passarelles	dried muscatel grapes
passe-crassane	a variety of very fragrant winter pear
passe-pierre	samphire, a type of seaside plant
passin	a cheese from Burgundy similar to gruyère
pastèque	watermelon
pastille	fruit or wine pastille
pastis	aniseed-flavoured apéritif; an apple cake
patates douces	sweet potatoes
pâte	pastry
pâté	terrine, pâté
pâte à chou	choux pastry, éclair pastry
pâte à frire	batter
pâte à pain	dough, bread-dough
pâte brisée	shortcrust pastry
pâte d'amandes	almond paste, marzipan
pâté de campagne	rough farmhouse pâté
pâte de coings	quince cheese/jam
pâté de foie	liver pâté
pâté de Pâques	Easter pie, chicken or rabbit pie
pâté en terrine	potted meat
pâté feuilletée	flaky pastry
patelle	an edible mollusc similar to a limpet
pâté maison	home-made pâté
pâté, petit	pasty, pielet
pâtes	pasta
pâtes alimentaires	pasta
pâtes fraîches	noodles, fresh pasta
pâtisseries	cakes, pastries
pâtissière, noix	round of veal, chump of veal
patisson	squash, vegetable marrow
patranque	Auvergne rarebit – a hot bread-and-cheese dish
pauchouse	a freshwater fish stew
Paulette, salade	with celery, potatoes, truffles, french beans

paupiette	slice of meat rolled, stuffed and gently braised
pavé	shaped in squares, slices
pavé d'Auge	a cheese from Auge
pavé de boeuf	steak, square-shaped cut
pavé de Moyaux	a cheese from Normandy
pavie	a firm-fleshed clingstone peach
pavot	poppy
pavot, graines de	poppy seeds
pa y all	garlic bread with salt and olive oil
paysanne	with assorted vegetables and sometimes bacon
pays, du	local, of the area
pebronata de boeuf	braised beef flavoured with juniper
pebronata de Provence	braised veal
pécari	wild pig
pêche	peach
pêches Bourdaloue	peach tart with frangipane cream
pêche Melba	vanilla ice-cream with fresh peaches and raspberry purée
peigne	pecten, scallop
pelamide	a fish related to tunny
pelardon de Ruoms	a goat cheese from the Ardèche
pelé	peeled, skinned
pellmènes	ravioli used as a garnish for soup, etc
pelouse	a fish
pelure	rind, skin, peelings
pelure d'oignon	dark rosé wine
pelvoux	a cheese from Dauphiné
perce-pierre	samphire, type of sea plant
perche	perch
perch de mer	sea-perch/bass
perchette	baby perch
perdreau	young partridge
perdrigon	plump variety of plum
perdrix	partridge
perdrix de neige	ptarmigan
périgourdine	with truffles and sometimes foie gras
périgueux	with truffles and Madeira wine
perle	pearl

perles, consommé de	thin soup with pearl barley
perlot	name for a small oyster
pernollet, salade	with crayfish, lettuce, truffles, asparagus tips
perpétuelle de Billard	variety of raspberry
persane	with aubergines, onions and tomatoes
persil	parsley
persil en pluches	sprigs of parsley
persillade	beef salad seasoned with parsley
persillé	with parsley
péruvienne	with oxalis and mixture of ham and chicken
pesto	a sauce made from olive oil and basil
pestou	garlic and basil butter
petarram	dish made from sheeps' tripe
petit	small
petit carré	a small, square cheese
petit duc	with asparagus, truffles and chicken tartlets
petit-gris	a type of tiny edible snail
petit lait	whey
petit pain	bread roll
petits fours	tiny fancy cakes and biscuits
petits pois	young garden peas
petit suisse	small cream cheese
pétoncle	small scallop
pets-de-nonne	soufflé fritters made from choux pastry
pic	woodpecker
picarel	small anchovy-like fish
pichet	small jug, pitcher
picholine	large elongated olive
picodon de Dieulefit	a cheese made in Dauphiné
pie	magpie
pièces de boeuf	braised beef; top rump of beef
pied	foot, trotter
pied de céleri	head of celery
pied de cheval	variety of large oyster
pied de laitue	head of lettuce
pied de porc	pig's trotter
pied de veau	calves' foot

pied-noir, cuisine de	Algerian cooking
pieds-paquets	Provençal dish containing tripe
pie grièche	shrike, small bird
piémontaise	with risotto and truffles; with potato and eggs
piémontaise, sauce	rich white sauce with onions, truffles, pine kernels
pigeon	pigeon
pigeonneau	young pigeon, squab
pignoli or pignon	pine seed, pine kernel
piguille	a creamy white curd cheese
pilaf	pilaff
pilate	variety of non-climbing raspberry
pilau	pilaff
pilé	crushed, ground
pilet	pintail duck
pilon	drumstick (of poultry)
piment	pimento, red pepper
pimenté	highly spiced
piments doux	sweet peppers
pimprenelle	salad burnet, a herb
pincée	pinch
pinée	first quality dried cod
pintade	guinea fowl
pintadeau	young guinea fowl
pinte	French pint (equal to an English quart)
piochou	variety of green cabbage
pipérade	Basque dish, comprising eggs, sweet peppers and vegetables, similar to an omelette; mixture of onions and tomatoes
piquage de viandes	interlarding of meat
piquant	sharp, tart taste
piquante, sauce	spicy sauce with gherkins
pirono	sea bream
pissaladière or pissaladière niçoise	an open onion and tomato tart garnished with anchovies or sardines and black olives
pissaladrina	an onion and olive tart from Provence

pissalat	a savoury purée
pissenlit	dandelion
pistache	pistachio
pistache de terre	peanut, ground nut
pistache, en	method of preparing mutton with a garlic garnish
pistole	a variety of plum used for drying
pistou	herb-flavoured paste
pistou, soupe au	soup made from tomatoes, garlic, basil, beans and vermicelli with various vegetables
pithiviers au foin	an Orléanais cheese ripened on hay
pithiviers, gâteau de	a puff pastry and almond gâteau
plaisir	small cone-shaped wafer biscuit
plaquemine	persimmon
plat	plate, dish
plat du jour	dish of the day, day's special dish
plein de	full of
pleurotte	an edible fungus; large field mushroom
plie or plie franche	plaice
plombière	an iced dessert
plouse	a fish similar to cod
pluches	leaves, sprigs
pluvier	plover
poché	poached
pochouse	a freshwater fish stew
pochteau	type of ray or skate with a pointed muzzle
poêlé	pot-roasted
pogne	a large tart filled with fruit, often pumpkin
pognon	a girdle cake made in Burgundy
pogne de romans	a type of sweet brioche
point, à	medium cooked (of steak)
poire	pear
poiré	perry, fermented pear-juice drink
poirée or poirée à carde	swiss chard, seakale beet
poireau	leek
poire de curé	variety of dessert pear
pois carrés	marrowfat peas

pois cassés	split peas
pois chiches or cornus	chickpeas
pois de Clamart	small peas eaten before they are fully grown
pois frais	new peas, fresh garden peas
pois mangetout	peas eaten complete with their pods
pois Michaux	small peas eaten before they are fully grown
pois, petits	fresh young peas
pois, purée de	pease pudding, thick pea soup
pois princesses	edible podded sugar peas
pois secs	dried peas
pois verts	green peas
poisson	fish
poissonaille	small fry
poisson-chat	cat-fish
poisson sauteur	regional name for grey mullet
poitrine	breast of lamb or veal; brisket of beef
poivrade	a highly seasoned sauce; young artichokes eaten with salt
poivrade, sauce	a rich brown sauce with onions, carrots and ham
poivre	pepper
poivré	pepper-flavoured, peppery
poivre d'âne	a cows'-milk cheese from the Riviera
poivre de cayenne	cayenne pepper, mild red pepper
poivre de Jamaïque	allspice
poivre, grains de	peppercorns
poivron	sweet pepper
poivron dou	sweet pepper
polenta	a type of maize-meal porridge
polonaise	with hard-boiled eggs, parsley and butter
polonaise, sauce	with horseradish and butter
polypore	a giant edible fungus
pommade	a thick paste of garlic, basil, cheese, olive oil
pomme	apple
pommé, chou	white heart cabbage
pomme de terre	potato

pommes	apples
pommes à couteau	eating apples
pommes au beurre	baked in butter
pommes au Chambertin	poached in Chambertin wine
pommes bonne femme	baked gently in water
pommes Bourdaloue	poached in syrup
pommes, compôte de	stewed, poached apples
pommes Figaro	with almonds and chestnuts
pommes Irène	with ice cream, prunes and meringue
pommes meringuées	apple snow
pommes sauvages	crab apples
pommes de terre	potatoes
pommes à la crème	sliced and served with cream
pommes à l'anglaise	plain boiled
pommes à la parisienne	cut into tiny nut shapes and fried in butter
pommes anna	casseroled in slices
pommes annette	casseroled in thin strips
pommes au four	baked potatoes
pommes boulangère	baked around a meat joint
pommes château	roasted
pommes chatouillard	ribbon-cut and fried
pommes chips	game chips, crisps
pommes copeaux	ribbon-cut
pommes crainquebille	steamed whole with onions, breadcrumbed and browned before serving
pommes dauphines	creamed, mixed with choux pastry, shaped in balls and deep fried
pommes duchesse	purée of potato and egg yolks, piped and baked
pommes en liards	potato crisps, game chips
pommes en robe des champs	potatoes baked in their skins
pommes fondantes	cut into egg shapes and shallow fried
pommes frites	chips, cut into finger sizes and deep fried
pommes frites pont neuf	English-style chips
pommes georgettes	baked in skins, centres removed and

	mixed with crayfish sauce and returned to skins
pommes lyonnaise	sliced and sautéed with onions
pommes macaire	creamed and baked in a deep anna mould
pommes maître d'hotel	boiled, sliced and cooked with milk and butter
pommes Mont-Doré	creamed with cheese, baked until browned
pommes nature	plain boiled or steamed
pommes noisettes	cut in nut-shapes and fried in butter
pommes pailles	straw potatoes, ie cut into matchstick-shapes and deep fried
pommes parmentier	cut into half-inch cubes and shallow fried
pommes purée	creamed with butter and milk
pommes vapeur	steamed
pompe	a traditional Christmas cake from Provence
pomponettes	small hot meat pasties eaten as an hors d'oeuvre
pontgibaud	a Roquefort-like cheese made from cows' milk
Pont l'Evêque	a medium strong creamy cheese from Normandy
ponts-neufs	pastries made with frangipane cream
porc	pork
porcelet	sucking pig
porc salé	pickled pork
porto	port
Port Royal, salade	with potatoes, apples, french beans, lettuce and hard-boiled eggs
Port Salut	medium strong creamy cheese from Normandy
portugaise	with tomatoes and mushrooms and garlic; a deep oyster
pot	little dish, ramekin
potage	a thick soup
potagère	from the casserole

potagères, herbes	pot-herbs
pot au chocolat	a chocolate cream dessert
pot-au-feu	beef broth; boiled beef and vegetables
potée	a casserole; a thick soup with meat, vegetables and beans or lentils
potiron	pumpkin
pot-pourri	a medley
pouchouse	a freshwater fish stew
poudin	pudding, especially suet pudding with raisins
poudin à l'anglaise	a sweet or savoury suet pudding
poudin de cabinet	a layered sponge, fruit and custard pudding
poudin de gibier	little game moulds usually with truffles
poudin de volaille	little poultry moulds with truffles
poudin diplomate	a pudding of sponge fingers and custard cream
poudre	powder
poudre d'amandes	finely ground almonds
pougny	a Burgundian cheese
pouillard	young partridge
poularde	fattened pullet, large hen
poule	fowl, chicken
poule à bouillir	a boiling fowl
poule au pot	boiled chicken
poule, lait de	egg-nog
poulet	chicken
poulet de Bresse	special chicken from Bresse
poulet de grain	grain-fed chicken
poulet en vessies	chicken sausages
poulette	young chicken
poulette, à la	a fricassee with cream, onions, mushrooms
poulette, sauce	with eggs, mushrooms, lemon juice and parsley
pouligny-Saint-Pierre	a cheese from Berry
pouliot	pennyroyal, a mint-flavoured herb
poulpe	octopus
poupelin	a choux pastry and cream gâteau
poupeton	a meat roll made from assorted meats

pourpier	purslane
pousse-café	liqueur, drink served with coffee
poussin	spring chicken
poutargue	dried mullet roe
poutine	small fry of fish
pragon	ruscus, an asparagus-like plant
praire	clam
pralin	toffee, caramel
praline	burnt almond caramel
praliné	usually caramelized walnut; an almond-flavoured sponge cake with praline butter cream
pratelle	a variety of edible mushroom
premier(ière)	first
pré salé, agneau de	lamb raised on salt meadow pastures
Président Carnot	variety of strawberry
pression, sous	draught (of beer)
prête	small seafish with delicate flesh
pretzel	savoury biscuit served with beer
primevère	primrose
Prince Albert	with whole truffles and sometimes foie gras
princesse	with asparagus tips, truffles and artichokes
princesse, sauce	white sauce with parsley, lemon juice and nutmeg
printanière	with a mixture of carrots, turnips, peas and beans
prix	price
prix fixe, menu	set price menu
profiterole	small choux pastry with sweet or savoury filling
provençale	with garlic, tomatoes, anchovies and herbs; with aubergines, tomatoes and beans
prune	plum
pruneau	prune, dried plum
prune de damas	damson
prune de la reine Claude	greengage
prune goutte d'or	golden drop plum

prunelle	sloe
puant macéré	cheese from the region of Nord
puits d'amour	pastries made from flaky pastry, cream-filled
purée	creamed; thick cream soup
purée, pommes	creamed potatoes
Puy-de-Dôme	cheese similar to Roquefort

quasi de veau	small pieces of leg of veal
quatre	four
quatre-épices	allspice
quatre mendiants	dessert of figs, raisins, nuts and almonds
quenelle	fish or meat ball rolled into sausage shape and steamed
quenelles de brochet	steamed pike balls
Quercy, bleu de	a blue cheese from the Dordogne
quetsche	small purple plum
queue	tail
queue de boeuf	ox-tail
queues d'écrevisses	crayfish tails
quiche	a pastry tart containing a savoury custard and various other ingredients
quiche lorraine	a tart made with smoked bacon, cream and eggs
quignon	a hunk of bread
quillet	a pastry cake filled with butter cream
quintal	a variety of cabbage
rabes de morue	salted cod roe
rabiole	a variety of kohl-rabi or turnip
râble	saddle
râble de lièvre	saddle of hare
rabotte	dumpling
rabotte de pomme	apple dumpling
rabotte, poire en	pear dumpling
Rachel	with bone-marrow and artichoke hearts

Rachel, salade	with artichokes, asparagus tips, celery
Rachel, purée	creamed artichoke hearts
raclette	a melted cheese dish, often with potatoes
radis	radish
radis noir	black radish
radis rose	red radish
raffiné, sucre	refined sugar
raffinées, friandises	choice dainties
ragot	a boar which is over two years old
ragoût	stew of meat, fowl or fish
ragoût de mouton	mutton stew
ragoute	agaric, an edible fungus
rahat loukoum	Turkish delight
raie	ray, skate
raifort	horseradish
rainette	pippin (apple). See reinette
raipouce	vegetable similar to salsify
raisin	grape
raisin de Corinthe	(dried) currants
raisin de Malaga	dried muscat grapes eaten for dessert
raisiné	fruit preserved in grape juice
raisin sec	raisin
raisin sec de Smyrne	sultana
raitou	small, young skate
râle	rail, a wading bird similar to quail
rambour	a variety of apple
ramequin	tart or tartlet filled with cream cheese or other filling; a little dish
ramereau	ring dove, young wood-pigeon
ramia or ramies	okra, ladies' fingers
ramier	wood pigeon
râpé	grated; grated cheese
Raphaël, salade	with lettuce, cucumber, asparagus tips, radishes and paprika flavoured mayonnaise
rascasse	hog-fish, scorpion-fish
rastègne	a small sea anemone
ratafia	an almond liqueur; tiny almond flavoured macaroon

ratatouille	stew of aubergines, tomatoes, courgettes and onions
rate	spleen
raton	pastry with a cream cheese basis
rave	rapeseed, coleseed
rave, céleri-	celeriac
ravigote	highly seasoned white cream sauce
raviole	small leaf-pastry savoury with cheese filling
ravioli	tiny pasta pillows filled with meat paste
rayon de miel	honeycomb
reblochon	a soft, ewes' milk cheese from Savoy
réchauffé	warmed up, re-heated
recollet de Gérardmer	a cheese from the Vosges area
recuite	a cheese made from whey
régence	garnished with meat or fish quenelles
régence, sauce	a chicken-based sauce with ham, onions and wine
réglisse	liquorice
reine	usually with chicken; spring chicken
reine-claude	greengage
reine des reinettes	variety of russet apple
reine des vergers	variety of elongated peach
reine pédauque, salade	with lettuce, fruit and mustard-flavoured mayonnaise
reinette de Canada	variety of yellow-coloured apple
reinette franche	fragrant variety of apple
reinette grise	firm, crisp variety of apple (russet)
réjane	with spinach, artichokes, bone-marrow and duchesse potatoes
réjane, salade	with asparagus tips, truffles and potatoes
religieuse	chocolate or coffee cream eclair; pastry tart with jam and currants
rémoulade	a sharp mayonnaise with capers, gherkins and herbs
renaissance	with a variety of spring vegetables
renne	reindeer, venison
Rennes mingaux	type of cream cheese from Brittany

repas	meal
repas de noces	wedding breakfast
repas, léger or petit	snack, light meal
requin	shark; also, a saltwater fish of the shark family
réveillon	midnight supper (particularly on Christmas or New Year's Eve)
rhubarbe	rhubarb
rhum	rum
Ricard	pastis, an aniseed-flavoured drink
ricart	variety of strawberry
riceys cendré	a Champenois cheese
richelieu	with tomatoes, lettuce, potatoes, mushrooms; egg and breadcrumbed fish garnished with truffles; a large sweet pastry containing almonds, egg white and frangipane cream
richelieu, sauce	rich white sauce with chicken glaze, onions and butter
ricin, huile de	castor oil
rigadelle	clam
rigarade	flavoured with bitter or Seville oranges
rigodon	a sweet or savoury baked custard
rigotte de Condrieu	a small, hard goat cheese
rigottes	goat cheese from Burgundy
rillauds, also rillettes	potted pork
rillons or rillots	potted pork
riommois	a small cheese from Auvergne
ris	sweetbreads
ris de veau	calves' sweetbreads
risotto	a savoury dish based on rice
rissole	rissole; small pastry turnover filled with forcemeat
ritz, fruits	strawberries with cream and a raspberry and strawberry purée
rivèle	dumpling
riz	rice
riz au lait	sweet rice pudding
riz, gâteau de	stiff sweet rice dessert
rizot	a savoury rice dish similar to risotto

riz, papier de	rice paper
Robert, sauce	with white wine, vinegar, onions, mustard
Rocamadour	a small ewes' milk cheese
rocambole	Spanish garlic, vegetable similar to shallots
rochambeau	with carrots, lettuce, cauliflower, anna potatoes
rognon	kidney
rognonade	saddle of veal or rabbit with the kidney attached
rognon de boeuf	ox kidney
rohan	with artichokes, fois gras, truffles, cocks' kidneys and cockscombs
roi de caille	land rail, a bird similar to quail
roitelet	fire-crested wren, small edible bird
rollot	small disc-shaped cheese from Picardy
romaine	cos lettuce
romaine	with gnocchi tartlets and spinach
Romalour	a cheese from the Loire district
Romanoff; Romanov	with cucumber, mushrooms and duchesse potatoes
Romanoff, fraises	strawberries in curaçao with cream
Romanoff, sauce	a game stock sauce with pine-kernels, sultanas, currants, caramel and vinegar
romarin	rosemary, a herb
romsteck, or rumsteck	rump steak
ronce	blackberry
ronce-framboise	loganberry
rondelle	ring, slice (of sausage, etc.)
Roquefort	a cheese made from ewes' milk
roquette	rocket cress, cress with very strong flavour
roquille	candied orange peel
rosbif	roast beef
rosé	pink wine, rosé
rosette	a special sausage from Lyons which is eaten raw
Rossini	with foie gras and truffles
rôt	roast meat

rôtengle	a freshwater, roach-like fish
rôti	roast meat; roasted
rôti à la broche	spit roast
rôti au fromage	dish with toasted cheese
rôtie	slice of roast meat
rôtie à l'anglaise	Welsh rarebit
rôti, pain	toast
rotisson	chub, a freshwater fish
rouelle	a round of lemon, beef, etc.; slice across joint
rouelle de veau	fillet of veal
rouennais	with ducks' livers and red wine; a Normandy cheese
rouennaise, sauce	with beef marrow and duck or chicken livers
rougail	a spicy condiment served with Creole dishes
rouge	red
rouge de rivière	type of wild duck
rouge-gorge	robin
rouge-queue	redstart, small game bird
rougeret	a small goats' cheese
rouget	red mullet; gurnet
rouille	a spicy dressing made from garlic, stale bread and chillies
rouille, sauce	with grilled peppers, lobster coral, sea urchins
roulade	rolled piece of meat; shaped in a roll; slice of meat stuffed and rolled
roulé	rolled-up biscuit, sometimes filled
rousette	a salmon-like fish; a type of fritter
rousselet	a variety of russet pear
rouville	a variety of pear
rouyat	an apple paste, dessert
royale	moulded custard used as garnish for clear soups
royan	variety of large sardine
rubané	in strips, layered
rubané de canard	duck terrine
Rubens, sauce	a fish sauce with anchovy essence,

	crayfish butter
russe, salade	mixed vegetable salad with tongue and/or crayfish
russe, sauce	mayonnaise with lobster and caviare purée
russule	russula, an edible fungus
rutabaga	swede

s.g.	(selon grosseur/grandeur), priced according to size or weight
sabayon	zabaglione, a very light cream mousse
sablé	a delicate cake or biscuit
sacristain	a small puff pastry
safran	saffron
sagan	with risotto, mushrooms, brains
sagou	sago
saignant	bloody, underdone (of meat)
saindoux	lard
Saint Agathon	a Breton cheese
Sainte-Maure	a soft, creamy goat cheese
Saint Emilion	pudding of macaroons with chocolate custard
St.Florentin	a fresh cream cheese from Burgundy
Saint Germain	with fresh green peas; thick pea soup
Saint-Honoré	gâteau containing cream-filled choux pastry buns
St.Hubert, consommé	a thin game soup garnished with mushrooms
St.Jacques, coquilles	scallops
Saint-Jean	a small early variety of pear
Saint-Loup	a cheese from the Poitou area
St.Malo, sauce	a sharp fish sauce with mustard, Worcester sauce
Saint-Mandé	with peas, beans and potatoes
St.Marcellin	a flat creamy cheese from the French Alps

Saint Marie	a cows'-milk cheese from the Loire Valley
Saint Michel	a coffee-flavoured layered gâteau
saint-pierre	a fish, John Dory
Saint Rémi	a soft, square cheese
Saint-Saëns	with tiny meat fritters
St.Yore	a sparkling spa water from the Vichy area
saison, de	when in season
salade	salad
salade Aïda	with chicory, artichokes, pimentos
salade bagatelle	with carrots, mushrooms, asparagus tips
salade canaille	with tomatoes, asparagus, bananas, rice, cream, celery
salade Carmen	with grilled and peeled red peppers and chicken
salade composée	mixed salad
salade Dalila	with bananas, apples and celery
salade favorite	with crayfish tails and white truffles
salade Florida	with lettuce and oranges and soured cream
salade hongroise	with cabbage, horseradish, bacon and potatoes
salade indienne	with rice, asparagus tips, apples, sweet pepper and curried cream or mayonnaise
salade Lorette	with lamb's lettuce, celery and beetroot
salade mignon	with shrimps, artichoke hearts, truffles, cayenne pepper
salade mimosa	with lettuce, oranges, grapes, bananas
salade niçoise	with french beans, tomatoes, potatoes, olives, anchovies
salade polonaise	with assorted diced vegetables, gherkins, potatoes and roll-mop herrings
salade russe	mixed diced vegetables in mayonnaise
salade Waldorf	with celeriac, apples, walnuts
salamander	sprinkled with butter-fried breadcrumbs

salambo	a small, choux pastry cake with cream filling
salami	an Italian pork sausage
salé	salted; preserved in brine
salée, eau	salt water, brine
salé, petit	pickled pork or ham
salicoques	prawns
salmigondis	a re-heated stew of various sorts of meats
salmis	a roast joint of game or poultry in a red wine sauce
salpicon	one or more ingredients diced in a sauce
salsifis	salsify
samaritaines	timbales of rice with braised lettuce
sandre	zander, river fish, pike-perch
sang	blood
sangivine	pancake-like mixture of onions, butter and chicken's blood
sanglier	wild boar
sanguine	variety of blood-orange
sanquette	a pancake-like mixture of onions, butter and chicken's blood
sansonnet	starling
sarasin	buckwheat
sarcelle	teal
sardalaise	with pounded hard-boiled egg yolks and cream, sieved truffles and armagnac; with potatoes and truffles
sarde	with rice balls, cheese, stuffed tomatoes, cucumbers
sardine	sardine, pilchard
sargasse	sargasso, a seaweed eaten as salad
sarlardaise	baked, sliced potatoes cooked with truffles
sarments, grillé aux	grilled over a fire of vine-wood
sarrasines	small buckwheat cakes, rice tartlets
sarriette	savory, a herb
sartadagnano	little fish cooked tightly together, turned like a pancake, sprinkled with vinegar and paprika

sassenage	a semi-hard, blue-veined cheese from Isère
sauce	sauce
sauce aïoli	garlic flavoured mayonnaise
sauce à l'estragon	with tarragon
sauce allemande	classic egg and cream sauce
sauce béarnaise	with egg yolks, white wine, shallots and tarragon
sauce blanche	white sauce
sauce bordelaise	brown sauce with wine, onions and herbs
sauce bourguignonne	brown sauce with herbs, wine and onions
sauce hollandaise	with egg yolks, butter and lemon juice
sauce mornay	white sauce with cheese
sauce Noilly	vermouth sauce
sauce raifort	horseradish
sauce rémoulade	mayonnaise with capers, gherkins and herbs
sauce soubise	a cream sauce with onions
sauce verte	mayonnaise with pounded cress, spinach and herbs
sauce vinaigrette	oil and vinegar dressing for salad
saucisse	sausage
saucisse d'Augsbourg	dried smoked pork sausage
saucisse de Francfort	frankfurter
saucisse de Strasbourg	sausage similar to frankfurter
saucisse de Toulouse	large sausage, usually grilled
saucisse madrilène	small pork, veal and sardine sausage tied in rings
saucisse plate	little flat sausage
saucisse rouge	Spanish sausage flavoured with paprika
saucisson	dry sausage which needs no further cooking
saucisson à cuire	a raw sausage which must be cooked
sauge	sage, a herb
saumon	salmon
saumon blanc	hake
saumonée, truite	salmon trout
saumonette	small, salmon-like fish

saumure	pickle, pickling brine
saupiquet	a wine sauce for accompanying ham, rabbit or waterfowl
saur	salted, smoked herring
saurel	long fish similar to mackerel
sauté	shallow fried
sauterelle de mer	squillfish, a crustacean
savarin	a yeast cake soaked in rum or other spirit
saveur	taste, flavour
savoyarde	with potatoes and gruyère cheese
saxonne, purée	purée of potatoes, turnips and onions
scabieuse	scabious
scare	parrot-fish
scarole	escarole, an endive-like salad
schifela	shoulder of pork with turnips
schnitzel or schnitzen	escallope of veal, egg and bread-crumbed and fried
scorsonère, or scorzonère	scorzonera, black salsify, oyster plant
sec, sèche	dry
séché	dried
sèche	a flat bread made with eggs and sugar
seicke	squid, cuttlefish
seigle	rye
seigle, pain de	rye bread
sel	salt
sel blanc	table salt
sel de mer	sea salt
selle	saddle
selle de mouton	saddle of mutton
selon grosseur	priced according to weight and/or size
seltz	soda water
semi-fredo	a fruit charlotte
semoule	semolina
sénevé	black mustard
sept	seven
septmoncel	a cheese made with a mixture of cows' and goats' milk from the Jura region
sept-oeil	lamprey, a fish
seray	a strong, herb-flavoured cheese

serge	with artichokes and ham
serpolet	wild thyme
serré	a strong, herb-flavoured cheese
serviette, à la	special dish served in a linen napkin
sésame	sesame
sétoise	vermicelli
sévigné	with lettuces, mushrooms, château potatoes
sicilienne	with stuffed tomatoes, rice and potato croquettes
sigui fumé	thin strips of smoked salmon
silure	wels, a freshwater fish
sirop	syrup
six	six
smitane, sauce	with onions and soured cream
sobronade	soup with pork, vegetables and beans
soda	soda water
soissons	small, white, haricot beans
soissonaise	with white bean purée or whole white haricots
soja	soy, soya
soja, fromage de	soya bean curd
soja, viande de	soya meat substitute
sole	sole, a fish
solette	very small sole-like fish
solférino	with shallots, butter and tomatoes
sommelier	wine waiter, butler
sophie	with ham, hard-boiled eggs and cream
sorbet	water ice made from fruit juices, liqueurs or wine
sorbet Colonel	lemon water-ice with vodka
sorbet dijonnaise	blackcurrant water-ice with cassis liqueur
sorbet normande	apple water-ice with calvados
sot l'y laisse	parson's nose, rump of a chicken
soubise, sauce	cream sauce with onions; purée of onions and rice
souchet, sauce	with white wine, leeks, carrots, celery
soucoupe	saucer
sou-fassum	stuffed cabbage cooked in a casserole

soufflé	a sweet or savoury dish lightened and thickened with beaten egg-white
soufflé champignons	mushroom soufflé
soufflé florentine	spinach soufflé
soufflé parmesan	cheese soufflé
soumaintrin	soft, yellow, strong-flavoured cheese from Burgundy
soupe	soup
soupe au lait	bread and milk
soupe grasse	soup made with milk
soupe maigre	vegetable soup
soupir de nonne	a choux pastry fritter
source, eau de	spring water
souris	knuckle (of mutton)
sous-fassoun	stuffed cabbage cooked in a casserole
souvarov or souvorov	cooked in an earthenware casserole with foie gras and truffles
soya	soy, soya
spatzellis	type of pasta
spatzle	type of pasta
spetzei	a cream dumpling
squale	large edible sea-water fish of the shark family
squille	squill-fish, a crustacean prepared like lobster
stachys	Japanese artichokes
steack haché	beefburger
sterlet	baby sturgeon
strasbourgeoise	with sauerkraut and fois gras
strisciule	a Corsican dish of goats' meat cured in the sun
stromatée	rudderfish, a delicately flavoured fish
strudel	a dessert made with noodle pastry, apples, currants and cinnamon
subric	creamed and formed into a ball or sausage shape before cooking – may be sweet or savoury
subric de semoule	flat semolina flan cut into small shapes
sucette	lollipop
sucre	sugar

sucré	sugared, sweetened
sucre à glace	icing sugar
sucre cristallisé	granulated sugar
sucre d'érable	maple sugar
sucre de raisin	grape sugar, glucose
sucre d'orge	barley sugar
sucre en morceaux	sugar loaves, lump sugar
sucre en poudre	caster sugar
sucre semoule	caster sugar
sucrée, tarte	a firm pastry-cream tart
sucre tiré	pulled sugar
sucrerie	sweets, confectionery
sucrin	a sugary melon
suède, navet de	swede
suédoise	a layered fruit jelly
suédoise, pouding	bread and butter pudding with candied fruits
suédoise, sauce	mayonnaise with apples, horseradish and mustard
suisse, petit	small cream cheese usually eaten with sugar
sultane	a large, elaborate pastry; with red cabbage and duchesse potatoes; with chicken forcemeat and truffle tartlets
supions	type of fish
supplément	extra charge
suprême	fillet or breast of poultry, game or fish
suprême, sauce	rich white sauce with chicken flavour
sur	sour, tart
sureau, baie de	elderberry
surette	sour, tart
surimi	crab
surmulet	red mullet
suze	a bright yellow, herb-flavoured apéritif

tablette	slab, cake (of chocolate)
taboulé	bulgar wheat
tacaud	variety of cod
tacon	young salmon
taliburs aux pommes	apples baked in pastry
talmouse	a cheese tartlet
Talleyrand	with macaroni, truffles, foie gras
Talleyrand, sauce	chicken-flavoured with truffles and tongue
tanagra, salade	with celery, tomatoes, bananas, sour cream
tapenade	a savoury purée made with anchovies and black olives
tartare	minced, chopped
tartare, sauce	sharp mayonnaise with onion and chives
tartare, steak	minced beef steak seasoned and served raw with raw egg yolk, capers, onion and parsley
tarte	open tart, flan
tarte alsacienne	an almond-flavoured latticed tart
tarte bourbonnaise	a rich cheesecake with butter
tartelette	tartlet, small pie
tarte tatin	an upside-down apple tart
tartine	buttered portion of bread
tartine de confiture	slice of bread and jam
tartine suisse	a flaky pastry square, with a glazed top and filled with cream
tassard	king-fish, a large, firm, white-fleshed sea fish

tasse	cup
taupe	large fish of the shark family
tende de tranche	topside (of beef)
tendon	tendon, knuckle
terrapène	turtle
terre-noix	earth-nuts which taste similar to chestnuts
terrine	a rough pâté, meat loaf
testard	chub, a freshwater fish
tétard	sucking kid, young goat
tête	head
tête de Maure or de More	a Dutch cheese
tête de nègre	chocolate covered, tennis-ball-sized meringue
tête de porc	pig's head
tête de veau	calf's head
tête de veau en tortue	mock turtle
tête, fromage de	brawn, pig's cheese
tête persillée	brawn with parsley
tétine	udder
tétine de veau	calf's udder
tétras	grouse
thé	tea
thé citron	lemon tea
thé de Ceylan	Indian tea
thé, salon de	tea-room
thénay	a cheese from the Loire valley area
thon	tuna, tunny-fish
thonine	Mediterranean variety of tuna fish; way of cooking veal which has been marinated for a long period before cooking
thourins	an onion-based soup
thym	thyme, a herb
tiède	tepid, luke-warm
tiède, salade	warm salad or salad with a warm dressing
tilleul	lime
timbale	preparation cooked and/or served in a pie-crust; a small cup-shaped mould

tinamou	partridge-like bird
tire	toffee, candy
tisane	an infusion
tisane de camomile	camomile tea
tisane d'orge	barley-water
tivoli	with asparagus, mushrooms, cocks' kidneys and combs
toast beurré	buttered toast
tocan	a salmon under one year old
tomate	tomato
tomates, sauce de	tomato sauce
tombe	gurnard
tôme or tomme	a creamy cheese
tôme au fenouil	fennel-flavoured creamy cheese
tôme aux raisins	a creamy cheese matured in grapes
tôme de sixt	a very hard cheese from Savoy
tomme or tôme	a creamy cheese
tomme aux noix	cream cheese with nuts
topinambour	Jerusalem artichoke
torpille	torpedo fish, fish similar to skate
torta	an aniseed-flavoured Corsican cake
tortue	turtle, or a dish served with veal quenelles, crayfish, olives and calves' brains
tortue de mer	turtle
tortue, sauce	a rich brown madeira and herb sauce
Tosca, salade	with chicken, truffles, celery, parmesan cheese and anchovy essence
toscane	with macaroni, foie gras and truffles
toulia	type of onion soup from the Pyrenees
toulousaine or toulouse	with chicken quenelles, sweetbreads and mushrooms
tourain	an onion, tomato, egg and milk soup served poured over bread and sprinkled with cheese
tourain périgourdin	onion soup from Périgord
Touraine, géline de	a small black fowl, speciality of the Loire
tourangelle	with french beans and flageolets
tourd	an insipid Mediterranean fish

tourin	a garlic, onion, tomato and milk soup
tournedos	fillet steak
tournedos chasseur	fillet steak with shallots, mushrooms, tomatoes
tournedos Rossini	fillet steak topped with pâté and Madeira sauce
tourte	a covered tart
tourte à la lorraine	a quiche with veal and pork
tourteau	large edible crab
tourteau fromagé	a fermented baked cheese mousse
tourterelle	turtle dove
tourtière	a meat pie; a raised chicken pie; a minced pork pie
toute-bonne	a variety of pear
toute-épice	allspice; pimiento
tranche	slice
tranches, en	sliced
tranche napolitaine	mixed flavour ice cream
traquet	wheatear, a small game bird
trebuc, lou	preserved goose or pork
Tredern, salade	with oysters, crayfish tails, asparagus tips and truffles
trempette	bread for dunking
tresse	plait or braid, a loaf
trigle	gurnet, species of fish
tripa	sheeps' intestines stuffed with herbs and spinach and tied up like black pudding
triperie	a shop specialising in tripe
tripes	tripe
tripes à la mode de Caen	tripe cooked slowly with onions, carrots, herbs, apples, cider and calvados
tripette	fried squares of sheeps' intestines
tripoux	stuffed sheeps' feet
tripous du Rouergue	lamb's tripe cooked with tomatoes, wine and ham
trognon	edible heart of fruit or vegetable
trois	three
trois étoiles	three star (of brandy)
tronçon	chunk, slab (usually of fish)

troô	a cheese from Touraine
trou normand	calvados or calvados-doused sorbet taken between courses
trouvillaise	with shrimps, mussels and mushrooms
Troyes	a soft creamy cheese similar to Camembert
truffade	potatoes cooked with bacon, garlic and a tôme or Cantal cheese
truffe	truffle
truffé	stuffed with truffles
truffe blanche	white truffle
trufflagé	with truffles added
truie de mer	hog-fish
truite	trout
truite arc-en-ciel	rainbow trout
truite au bleu	fresh trout cooked in wine and vinegar which gives it a slightly blue appearance
truite commune	common trout
truite de Dieppe, or truite de mer	sea trout, salmon trout
truite de rivière	river trout
truite de torrent, or truite ruisseau	stream trout
truite saumonée	salmon trout
trumeau	leg of beef, skirt of beef
ttoro	a Basque fish stew
tuiles	small almond biscuits
tulipe	tulip
turban	food arranged in a circle
turbot	turbot
turbotin	chicken turbot, very small turbot
turbot lisse	brill
Tvarogue	with butter and cream cheese
tyrolienne	with tomatoes and onion rings
tzarine	with shaped cucumbers and cream

un(e)	one
uranoscope	small species of fish used in bouill-abaisse (i.e. fish stew)
vacherin	a soft cows'-milk cheese from Jura; a meringue ring filled with fruit and cream
vairon	minnow, small freshwater fish
Vallée d'Auge	with calvados, apples and cream
valence	Valencia orange
valençay	a goats'-milk cheese from the Loire Valley
valencienne	with rice and sweet peppers
valesniki	little cheese balls
valois	with potatoes and artichoke hearts
vandoise	dace, a freshwater fish
vanille	vanilla
vanneau	lapwing, peewit, plover
vanneaux, oeufs de	plovers' eggs
vapeur	steam
vapeur, pommes	steamed potatoes
varié(s)	varied, assorted
veau	veal
veau en vessie	veal sausages
veau, gelée de pieds de	calves' foot jelly
veau, ris de	calves' sweetbreads
veau, tête de	calf's head
végétarien(ne)	vegetarian
velouté	a thick, rich, sauce or soup

venaison	venison
venaison, basse	hare, rabbit
vendôme	variety of ewes'-milk cheese, can be hard or soft
ventadour	with marrow, truffles and artichoke purée
verdette	russula, edible fungus
verjus	verjuice, grape juice
vermicelle	vermicelli
vernon	with artichokes, asparagus, turnips, pea purée
véron, sauce	rich, strongly-flavoured veal sauce with cayenne, chervil and tarragon
verre	glass
vert	green
vert bonnet	verdette, an edible fungus
verte, salade	green salad
verte, sauce	mayonnaise with pounded watercress or spinach
vert-pré, au	with watercress and straw potatoes; with peas, beans and asparagus
verts, haricots	french beans
verts, légumes	green vegetables
verveine	verbena
vésiga	dried spine marrow of the sturgeon
vessie, en	sausages
viande	meat
viande de cheval	horsemeat
Vichy	a sparkling spa water
vichy	with carrots
Victoria	with macaroni, tomatoes, lettuces; with mushrooms, artichokes and stuffed tomatoes
Victoria, sauce	lobster sauce with chopped truffles; rich brown sauce with port, redcurrant jelly and orange peel
Vienne chabichou	a cheese from the Poitou area
viennois, beignets	deep fried, redcurrant-jelly filled brioche paste

viennoise	with noodles, spinach and celery; with chopped hard-boiled egg, capers, anchovies, olives and parsley
vigneronne, salade	with lettuce, stoned grapes and sour cream with lemon juice
vignette and vignot	Breton names for a winkle
villedieu	a cheese from Normandy
Villeroi, sauce	a thick sauce, flavoured with ham and truffles
vin	wine
vinaigre	vinegar
vinaigrette	with oil and vinegar dressing
Vincent, sauce	mixed tartare and green sauces
vin chaud	mulled wine
vin de Bordeaux	claret
vin de table	ordinary (house) wine
vin du Rhin	hock
vin mousseux	sparkling wine
vin ordinaire	ordinary/table wine
vin rosé	pink wine
vin rouge	red wine
Vincent, sauce	tartare sauce and green sauce mixed together
vingt	twenty
violettes, soufflé	soufflé decorated with crystallized violets
virgouleuse	variety of winter pear
viroflay	with spinach balls, artichoke quarters and château potatoes
Vittel	a still spa water
vive	weever fish, firm-fleshed fish
viverais de Picodon	a small, strong, goat cheese
viveurs, consommé	duck flavoured clear soup, with celery
viviane, potage	cream of chicken soup with artichokes and carrots
Vladimir	with cucumbers and diced courgettes
voilé	covered in spun sugar
voisin, pommes	anna potatoes with grated cheese
volaille	poultry, fowl

volaille, gelée de   cold jellied chicken soup
vol-au-vent   flaky pastry case with variable filling
vrac   wholesale, in bulk

wagon-bar	refreshment car
wagon-restaurant	dining-car
waldorf, salade	with celery, apples, bananas, walnuts, mayonnaise
walewska	with crayfish tails and truffles
wallace or fontaine wallace	drinking fountain
Washington	with sweetcorn and cream
waterfisch	freshwater fish
waterzoi or waterzooi	a thick freshwater fish or chicken soup or stew
Wilhelmine, fruits	kirsch-soaked strawberries, served with orange, sugar and whipped cream
William	a variety of pear
Windsor, salade	with celery, raw truffles, chicken, tongue, mushrooms and piccallili
winterthur	with peeled shrimps and crayfish
witloof	Belgian variety of endive
xérès	sherry
xérès, vin de	sherry
yahout	yoghurt
yam yam, salade	with french beans, cucumber, celeriac and lettuce
yaourt	yoghurt
Yorkshire, sauce	a port wine sauce with redcurrant jelly and thin slices of orange peel

zandre	zander, a pike-like fish
zampino	stuffed trotter or leg of pork
zee forgeron	John Dory, a fish
Zelma Kuntz	strawberries with raspberry purée and praline
zewelewai	an Alsation onion flan
zingara	with julienne of ham, tongue and truffles
zucchini	courgettes, baby marrows
zwieback	a variety of rusk, biscuit

DRINKS

Absinthe	an aniseed-flavoured apéritif
aigre de cidre	a citrus fruit drink
alcool	alcohol
alcool blanc	fruit brandy
améléon	a cider from Normandy
anisette	liqueur flavoured with aniseed
apéritif	drink taken before a meal
armagnac	a brandy from Gascony
babeurre	buttermilk
badianne	a strong, aniseed-flavoured spirit
Badoit	a sparkling spa water from Evian
bière	beer
bière blonde	pale ale
bière sans alcool	alcohol-free beer
bière sous pression	draught beer
bière de gingembre	ginger-beer
brut	dry
boisson	drink
byrrh	a wine-based apéritif
bénédictine	a liqueur containing brandy and herbs
cacao	cocoa
café (noir)	coffee (black)
café au lait	coffee with milk
café express	expresso coffee
café filtre	filtered coffee
calvados	apple brandy
cassis	a blackcurrant liqueur
chartreuse	a herbal liqueur
chaud(e)	hot, warm

chocolat (chaud/froid)	chocolate (hot/cold)
cidre bouché	bottled cider
citron vert	lime
citronnade	a still lemon drink
cognac	brandy
cognac trois étoiles	three-star brandy
consommation	drink
Contrexéville	a still spa water
crème de menthe	a peppermint liqueur
curaçao	liqueur made from Seville oranges
demi-sec	medium-dry (of wine)
Dubonnet	a wine-based apéritif
décafeiné	decaffeinated
eau	water
eau de vie	brandy
eau en carafe	tap water
eau minérale	mineral water
eau rougie	water with a dash of wine
épicéa	a pine-flavoured liqueur from the Jura
étrier	a stirrup-cup, hot drink
Evian	a still spa water
Express	espresso coffee
fenouillet	an aniseed-flavoured liqueur
fine	a quality brandy
fraise	strawberry brandy
frappé	chilled, on ice
froid	cold
gazeuse	aerated, fizzy
genévrette	juniper wine
glaçon	ice-cube
gniole	rum, brandy
grenadine	a very sweet fruit syrup
grog	a toddy
guignolet	cherry brandy
Izarra	a herb and flower liqueur
jus d'orange	orange juice
jus de fruits	fruit juice
jus de lime	lime juice
jus de pamplemousse	grapefruit juice
kir	a blackcurrant and wine cocktail

kir royal	kir made with champagne
kirsch	a cherry-flavoured liqueur
lait	milk
lait battu	buttermilk
lait de poule	egg-nog
laitiat	a drink of fruits mixed with whey
limonade	fizzy lemonade
madère	madeira wine
marc	a rough brandy
Marie Brizard	an aniseed-flavoured liqueur
Michelaine	liqueur made at Mont St Michel
mousseux	sparkling, fizzy
non-gazeuse	still
orange pressée	fresh squeezed orange juice
orangeade	fizzy orange drink
orangina	a fizzy orange drink
parfait-amour	lemon, cinnamon and coriander flavoured liqueur
pastis	an aniseed-flavoured apéritif
Pernod	an aniseed-flavoured apéritif, a pastis
pichet de vin	jug of ordinary (house) wine
poire	pear brandy
porto	port wine
pousse-café	a liqueur, drink served with coffee
pression	draught beer
rhum	rum
Ricard	an aniseed-flavoured apéritif, a pastis
salon de thé	tea-room, tea-shop
sans alcool	alcohol-free
seltz	soda water
soda	soda water
St. Yorre	a sparkling spa water from the Vichy area
suze	a bright yellow, herb-flavoured apéritif
tasse	cup
thé	tea
thé citron	lemon tea
thé de camomile	camomile tea
thé de Ceylan	Indian tea
thé, salon de	tea-room, tea-shop

tisane	an infusion (of herbs etc.)
tisane d'orge	barley water
une fine	brandy
verjus	grape-juice
verre	a glass
viandox	meat-extract drink (similar to Bovril)
Vichy	a sparkling spa water
vin blanc	white wine
vin chaud	mulled wine
vin de table	ordinary wine, house wine
vin de xérès	sherry
vin du Rhin	hock (wine)
vin rosé	pink wine, rosé
vin rouge	red wine
vin sec	dry wine
Vittel	a still spa water
xérès	sherry

Summary of English-French Terms

aerated/fizzy: gazeux

alcohol: l'alcool (*m*)

almonds: les amandes (*f*)

almonds, salted: les amandes salées

anchovy: l'anchois (*m*)

apple: la pomme

apricot: l'abricot (*m*)

artichoke: l'artichaut (*m*)

asparagus: les asperges (*f*)

avocado pear: l'avocat (*m*)

baked custard: la crème caramel

banana: la banane

bean stew: le cassoulet

beans, broad: les fèves (*f*)

beans, haricot: les haricots (*m*)

beef: le boeuf

beef, skirt: la bavette

beefsteak: le biftek/bifteck

beer: la bière

beer, draught: la bière sous pression

beer, non-alcoholic: la bière sans alcool

beer, pale ale: la bière blonde

beetroot: la betterave

beetroot soup: le bortsch

blackcurrant: le cassis

blue/blue cheese: bleu

brains: les cervelles (*f*)

braised: braisé

brandy: armagnac/cognac/eau de vie

brawn: le fromage de cochon

bread: le pain

bread, long thin loaf: la baguette/ficelle

bread roll: le petit pain

bread, rye: le pain de seigle

breadcrumbed: gratiné

breakfast: le petit déjeuner

bream: la brème

broccoli: le brocoli

Brussels sprouts: les choux de bruxelles (*m*)

bulgar wheat: taboulé

butter: le beurre

buttermilk: le babeurre

cabbage: le chou

cabbage, pickled: la choucroute

cabbage, red: le chou rouge

cake: le gâteau

cakes/pastries: les pâtisseries (*f*)

calves' sweetbreads: le ris de veau

139

caper: la câpre
capon: le chapon
caramel custard: la crème
    brûlée
carp: la carpe
carrot: la carotte
cauliflower: le choufleur
celeriac, celery roots: le céleri-
    rave
celery: le céleri
charcoal: le charbon
cheese: le fromage
cheese, blue: le fromage bleu
cheese, cream: le fromage à la
    crème
cheese, goats' milk: le fromage
    de chèvre
cherry: la cerise
chervil: le cerfeuil
chicken: le poulet
chickpeas: les pois chiches (m)
chicory: l'endive (f)
chilled, on ice: frappé
chips/french fries: les frites (f)
chocolate: le chocolat
chop, cutlet: la côte/côtelette
cider: le cidre
clam: la clovisse
clear soup/stock: le consommé
coconut: la noix de coco
cod: le cabillaud
coffee: le café
coffee with milk: le café au
    lait
coffee, black: le café noir
cold: froid
confectionery/preserves: la
    confiserie
cornflour: la farine de maïs
courgettes/baby marrows: les

courgettes
crab: le crabe
cranberry: le canneberge
crayfish: la langouste
crayfish tails: les queues
    d'écrevisses (f)
cream: la crème
cream, slightly soured: la
    crème fraîche
cream, whipped: la crème
    chantilly
creamed potatoes: les pommes
    purée (f)
creamed/thick cream soup: la
    purée
cucumber: le concombre
currant: la groseille
curry: le cari/currie
dab lemon sole: la limande
date: la datte
decaffeinated: décaféiné
diabetic: diabétique
dinner/to dine: diner
dish of the day: le plat du jour
drink: la boisson
dry: sec/sèche
Dublin Bay prawns/scampi: la
    langoustine
duck: le canard
eel: l'anguille (f)
egg: l'oeuf (m)
egg custard: la crème anglaise
eggplant: l'aubergine (f)
endive: la chicorée
endive, curly: la chicorée
    frisée
faggots: les crépinettes (f)
fennel: le fenouil
fig: la figue
fillet steak: le tournedos (m)

fillet sirloin cut: **le filet**
fillet slice of breast: **le magret**
fish: **le poisson**
fish or meat ball: **la quenelle**
fish soup or stew: **la bouillabaisse**
fizzy: **gazeux**
flamed in brandy: **flambé**
flavour/perfume: **le parfum**
flour/meal: **la farine**
fowl/chicken: **la poule/le
poulet**
frankfurter: **la saucisse de
francfort**
french beans: **les haricots verts
(m)**
French loaf: **la baguette/ficelle**
fritter: **le beignet**
frog: **la grenouille**
frogs' legs: **les cuisses de
grenouilles (f)**
fruit: **le fruit**
fruit brandy: **l'alcool blanc (m)**
fruit salad: **la macédoine de
fruits**
game: **le gibier**
game stew: **le civet**
garlic: **l'ail (m)**
gherkin: **le cornichon**
giblets: **les abatis (m)**
ginger: **le gingembre**
ginger-beer: **la bière de
gingembre**
goat: **la chèvre**
goats' milk cheese: **(fromage
de) chèvre**
goose: **l'oie (f)**
goose liver: **le pâté de foie
gras**
gooseberry: **la groseille**

grape: **le raisin**
grapefruit: **le pamplemousse**
green: **vert**
greengage: **la reine-claude**
grocer's shop: **l'épicerie (f)**
guinea fowl: **la pintade**
haddock:
**l'aiglefin/églefin/égrefin
(m)**
hake green pollack: **le colin**
halibut: **le flétan**
ham: **le jambon**
hare: **le lievre**
hazelnut: **la noisette**
herbs: **les herbes (f)**
herring: **le hareng**
honey: **le miel**
horse: **le cheval**
horseradish: **le raifort**
hot/warm: **chaude(e)**
ice cream, mixed: **la tranche
napolitaine**
ice cube: **le glaçon**
ice-cream/glaze: **la glace**
jam/marmalade: **la confiture**
Jerusalem artichoke: **le
topinambour**
juice/gravy: **le jus**
kebabs/skewer: **la brochette**
kidney: **le rognon**
lamb: **l'agneau (m)**
lamb stew: **le navarin**
leek: **le poireau**
leek tart: **la flamiche**
leg (of mutton): **le gigot**
lemon: **le citron**
lemon juice drink: **le citron
pressé**
lemonade: **la limonade**
lentils: **les lentilles (f)**

lettuce: la laitue
lime: le citron vert
liver: le foie
liver pâté: le pâté de foie
lobster: le homard
loin of pork: le carré de pore
lunch/luncheon: le déjeuner
mackerel: le maquereau
maize/sweetcorn: le mais
marrowbone: l'os à moelle (m)
meat: la viande
meat (or fish) ball: la boulette
meat loaf: la terrine
meats, cold: la charcuterie
meats, plate of assorted: l'assiette anglaise (f)
milk: le lait
mushroom: le champignon/
   cèpe
mussels: les moules (f)
mustard: la moutarde
mutton: le mouton
nectarine: le brugnon
nut/walnut: la noix
oil: l'huile (f)
olive: l'olive (f)
onion: l'oignon (m)
onion, green: la cive
orange drink, fizzy: l'orangina
   (f)
orange juice: le jus d'orange
ox-tail: la queue de boeuf
oyster: l'huitre (f)
pancake: la crépe
parsley: le persil
partridge: la perdrix
pasta: les pates (f)
pastis: l'absinthe/Pernod/
   Ricard

peach: la pêche
peanut/groundnut: la cachuète
pear: la poire
peas: les petits pois (m)
pepper: le poivre
pheasant: le faisan
pig's cheese/brawn: le fromage
   de téte
pig/pork: le cochon
pike: le brochet
pineapple: l'ananas (m)
plaice/flounder: le carrelet
plate/plateful: l'assiette (f)
plum: la prune
pork: le porc
pork/potted: les rillettes (f)
port: le porto
potato: les pommes/pommes
   de terre
potato crisps: les chips
poultry/fowl: la volaille
prawn: le bouquet
prune/dried plum: le pruneau
pumpkin: la citrouille, le
   potiron
quail: la caille
rabbit: le lapin
radish: le radis
raspberry: la framboise
ray/skate: la raie
rhubarb: la rhubarbe
rib of beef: la côte de
   boeuf/entrecôte
rib/Porterhouse steak: le
   contrefilet
rice: le riz
rissole/ball-shaped item: la
   croquette
rum: le rhum

rump steak: le romstek
rye: le seigle
rye bread: le pain de seigle
saddle of hare: le râble de
    lièvre
saddle of mutton: la selle de
    mouton
salad: la salade
salmon: le saumon
salmon trout: la truite
    saumonée
salt: le sel
salt-free: sans sel
sauerkraut: la choucroute
sausage: le saucisse/le saucis-
    son
saveloy/pork sausages: le
    cervelas
scallops: les coquilles St.
    Jacques (f)
scrambled: brouillé
sea crayfish/spiny lobster: la
    langouste
sea perch/dace/bass: le bar
seafood: les fruits de mer (f)
shallot/scallion: l'échalote (f)
sheep/mutton: le mouton
shellfish: les coquillages (f)
shrimps/prawn: les crevettes (f)
sirloin/porterhouse steak: le
    faux filet
slice: la tranche
small: petit
smoked/cured: fumé
snail: l'escargot (m)
snipe: la bécassine
soda: la seltz
sorrel: l'oseille (f)
soup: la soupe

spinach: les épinards (m)
spit-roasted: á la broche
spring chicken: le poussin
squid/inkfish: le calmar
stew/stock-pot: la marmite
stewed or poached fruits: le
    compôte de fruits
still (non-fizzy) drink: non-
    gazeux
strawberry: la fraise
sugar: le sucre
sweet chestnut: le marron
sweet pepper: le poivron
sweetbreads: le ris
sweetbreads, calves': le ris de
    veau
sweetcorn: le maïs
tea: le thé
tea, Indian: le thé de Ceylan
tea, lemon: le thé citron
tea-room: le salon de thé
terrine: le pâté
tomato: la tomate
tomato sauce: la sauce de
    tomates
tongue: la langue
tripe: les tripes (f)
trout: la truite
tuna/tunny-fish: le thon
turkey: la dinde/le dindon
turnip: le navet
vanilla: la vanille
varied/assorted: variés
veal: le veau
vegetable: le légume
vegetable mould: la chartreuse
    de légumes
vegetable salad: la macédoine
    de légumes

vegetarian: le/la végétarien(ne)
venison: la venaison/le
  chevreuil
vinegar: le vinaigre
water: l'eau (*f*)
water ice: le sorbet
water, bottled: l'eau minérale
  (*f*)
watercress: le cresson

white: blanc
whitebait: les blanchailles
wholemeal/wholewheat: le bis
wine, house: le vin de table
wine, red: le vin rouge
wine, white: le vin blanc
winkle: le bigorneau
woodcock: la bécasse
yoghurt: le yahout/yaourt